Acclaim for *Redbone Coonhound*

Winner of six METAs (Montreal English Theatre Awards), including Outstanding New Text, and nominated for five others

One of the *Toronto Star*'s "Ten Best Theatre Shows in 2023"

Biting, funny, and complex.
—BROADWAY WORLD

The play unpeels layer after layer of the complexities of race, racism, relationships, identity, power, privilege, sexism, feminism, misogyny, justice, rights, hypocrisy, language, culture, love, and family. Yes, it's a *lot*, but ... *Redbone Coonhound* successfully and meaningfully touches on each and every one of those subjects without ever coming across as preachy or self-righteous; rather, so many rapid-fire moments hit the heart hard, catch you, and make you think while you're laughing out loud ... it is likely the most fun you'll have this year confronting terrible and terribly pervasive truths.
—GAIL JOHNSON, *STIR*

A razor-sharp, intense, dramatic, and often hilarious commentary ... *Redbone Coonhound* invites us to mean what we say and say what we mean.
—OUR THEATRE VOICE

[An] innovative and compelling work ... *Redbone Coonhound* is a brilliantly fascinating look at race, sexism, and the power of words ... This play is absolutely genius.
—A VIEW FROM THE BOX

T0150751

REDBONE
COONHOUND

A PLAY BY

AMY LEE LAVOIE
AND
OMARI NEWTON

Teacher Resource Guide Included

TALONBOOKS

that I wouldn't have to deal with them anymore. I didn't play the popularity game, like so many people did. But I knew enough to alienate as few people as possible, especially those who could do damage. High school was a dangerous place. It can make or break a person and I can think of several who attended my prom night who are probably drug addicts or serial killers by now.

Children can be cruel, without knowing quite how or why, but teenagers can be even crueller, and they ought to know better. I have personal experience here. If there's one thing that I am grateful to my parents for, it was teaching me to try to be kind. My father had many chips on his shoulders, but he always instilled in me the belief that you should try to be nice. But if all else failed, take no prisoners. I guess that's why I had a rep at school for being a little fierce. But I wasn't. I guess I didn't care as much as others about being liked. A few close friends were enough for me, and I didn't have much time for the girls who just wanted to be popular for the sake of being popular. That didn't seem to make much sense to me, at the time. I think I understand it better now though. Hindsight is a wonderful thing.

Susan, x

Howard Manfred <rightsaidmanfred@qmail.com>
to: <soupy@qmail.com>   Apr 21, 2023, 12.04 PM

I agree with you on the hindsight issue, Susan, and I look back on my school days with some regret. I feel I could have done better and learnt more, but I also feel that my teachers didn't make learning as interesting or as much fun as it could have been. I learn so much from you, for example, and I love researching the things you write about that I don't understand, because if you know something, I want to know it too. You make learning fun, and I look forward to it. I want to match you, although I doubt I will ever be able to, but at least I want to hold my own.

This kind of thing didn't seem to matter very much to me when I was at school. There weren't enough teachers who seemed to care about whether their pupils were learning or not. It was just a job to some of them, and you could tell the ones who were just going through the motions. And you could also tell the ones who weren't. My English teacher, for example, Mr Newell, I think his name was. Yes, Newell, first name Alan (or maybe Allan, or Allen, not sure). Now he made lessons fun, and stimulating. I looked forward to them. It was almost as though he was able to relate to us and knew what we wanted to hear or what would interest us. It was as though he knew that being a schoolboy wasn't easy and he was trying to help by not boring the crap out of us.

Talonbooks
9259 Shaughnessy Street, Vancouver, British Columbia, Canada V6P 6R4
talonbooks.com

Talonbooks is located on xʷməθkʷəy̓əm, Sḵwx̱wú7mesh, and səlilwətaɬ Lands.

First printing: 2024

Typeset in Minion
Printed and bound in Canada on 100% post-consumer recycled paper

Talonbooks acknowledges the financial support of the Canada Council for the Arts, the Government of Canada through the Canada Book Fund, and the Province of British Columbia through the British Columbia Arts Council and the Book Publishing Tax Credit.

Rights to produce *Redbone Coonhound*, in whole or in part, in any medium by any group, amateur or professional, are retained by the authors. Interested persons are requested to contact Rena Zimmerman, Great North Artists Management Inc.: 350 Dupont Street, Toronto, Ontario, M5R 1V9, (416) 925-2051, renazimmerman@gnaminc.com.

Library and Archives Canada Cataloguing in Publication

Title: Redbone coonhound : a play / Amy Lee Lavoie and Omari Newton.
Names: Lavoie, Amy Lee, author. | Newton, Omari, author.
Identifiers: Canadiana 20230528538 | ISBN 9781772016147 (softcover)
Subjects: LCGFT: Drama.
Classification: LCC PS8623.A83555 R44 2024 | DDC C812/.6—dc23

For you

DUAL DRAMATURGIES

In the middle of rehearsals for *Redbone Coonhound,* during an elevator ride, someone asked me about the play: What is it? What is it about? Where does that title come from? and, most notably, What is the theme of the play? Dutifully, I offered a variety of themes we engaged with over four years of developing the script: racial micro-aggression, cultural conflict, and language inadequacy. But as I clumsily stumbled around in trying to answer this seemingly simple question, the short elevator ride was over. It's just as well – I clearly needed more time to properly articulate the answer to myself.

When Amy Lee and Omari first told me about their idea for this script, I was deeply drawn to its playful audacity and bold approach to dramatic structure, yet curious about the narrative challenges it would present. While supporting the project through an audio play recording and two onstage productions, I began to see that the beautiful, curious tone of their remarkable script is rooted in its contradictions and its binaries. If we consider the main narrative of the play – what we call the "throughline" or the "spine" (the story of Mike, Marissa, and their friends) – it's a rather clear, chronological plot. However, with the inclusion of the satirical "fever dream" scenes, which are sidesteps away from the narrative spine, we venture into structural unfamiliarity; we might struggle a bit to reconcile these two dramaturgies. But perhaps that is the play's superpower.

After the opening scene in which Marissa and Mike meet the titular dog during an afternoon walk, we "follow the dog" into a completely different world – one that appears to be a satirical version of the antebellum south. It's disorienting and creates a sense of estrangement – it kinda pushes us away a little bit and we must renegotiate what kind of play we are watching: "What is this? I thought it was a play about an interracial couple." But the scene is intriguing, and there might even be something about it that we feel we've seen before somewhere. Next, when we are brought back to Marissa and Mike's home, a more comfortable familiarity is restored ("Cool, these two again. They're talking about the dog. I remember the dog. That was fucked up."). But then we "follow the dog" to a 1930s Hollywood soundstage. Again: very disorienting, but somewhat familiar ("Have I seen something like this on YouTube?"). By this point, we accept that the play has the potential to do almost anything, take us anywhere – it draws on a variety of well-known tropes, like ones from *Star Trek* and *Guess Who's Coming to Dinner* – yet it will always return us back to Marissa and Mike's life.

The play's consistent reliance on intertextual references to prior cultural narratives – to movies, to TV shows, to YouTube clips – nurtures an enduring (yet shifting) sense of familiarity. When delivered to us in an unfamiliar and potentially puzzling macrostructure of alternating throughlines and fever-dream scenes, the result is a remarkable push-pull effect: the play both sets us at a distance and pulls us in. It expands and contracts in a repeated breathing pattern, and we find our expectations both confirmed and challenged in appropriate measures. The play's dual dramaturgy can have us saying to ourselves "What is going on?" *and* "I know exactly what's going on" *at the same time.* If we accept the beautiful premise that a play is a machine for creating meaning, *Redbone Coonhound* does so by offering an experience that is rooted in a binary of debates, arguments, and dialectical exploration.

And in terms of theme: far from being a pat, brief, fortune-cookie aphorism that an otherwise semi-articulate dramaturg can share during an elevator ride, perhaps the theme of this play is the result of a deep, meaningful conversation with and within each audience member – one rooted in a multiplicity of perspectives, a variety of intertextual relationships, and the rhythm of collective breath.

—STEPHEN DROVER

Dramaturg, Vancouver, May 2023

PRODUCTION HISTORY

Redbone Coonhound was commissioned by the Arts Club Theatre Company, Vancouver, British Columbia, as a part of its Silver Commissions Program. It was first produced by the Arts Club Theatre (as part of a rolling world premiere with Tarragon Theatre and Imago Theatre) on the Newmont Stage at the BMO Theatre Centre in Vancouver from October 12 to 30, 2022, with the following cast and crew:

JOGGER 1/STILL/MR. JIMMY/GERALD/ COMRADE BLACKITY BLACK:	Kwesi Ameyaw
JOGGER 2/ZAC/JORDAN/JAMAL:	Sebastien Archibald
CAMILLE/JENNIFER/MOM/KAREN:	Nancy Kerr
MIKE/GLIB/TOM:	Jesse Lipscombe
JEFFREY/DOLLEY/PRODUCER/ DAD/ROGER:	Gerry Mackay
JOGGER 3/AISHA/HARRIET TUBMAN /COMRADE BLACK:	Emerjade Simms
MARISSA/MISS SUE/ALICE:	Emma Slipp

Co-Directors:	Omari Newton and Ashlie Corcoran
Assistant Director:	Jessie Liang
Dramaturg:	Stephen Drover
Set Designer:	Kevin McAllister
Costume Designer:	CS Fergusson-Vaux
Lighting Designer:	Jonathan Kim
Sound Designer:	Owen Belton
Projection Designers:	Chimerik Collective 似不像: Sammy Chien and Caroline MacCaull
Movement Director:	Ghislaine Doté
Tap Choreographer:	Troy McLaughlin
Fight Director:	Jonathan Hawley Purvis
Dialect Coach:	Alison Matthews
Stage Manager:	Yvonne Yip
Assistant Stage Manager:	Victoria Snashall

The play was subsequently co-produced by Tarragon Theatre, Toronto, Ontario, and Imago Theatre, Montréal, Québec, as part of the rolling world premiere. It ran at Tarragon Theatre from February 7 to March 5, 2023, and at Théâtre Denise-Pelletier from March 21 to April 1, 2023, with the following cast and crew:

JOGGER 1/STILL/MR. JIMMY/GERALD/ COMRADE BLACKITY BLACK	Kwesi Ameyaw
JOGGER 2/ZAC/JORDAN/JAMAL	Jesse Dwyre
CAMILLE/JENNIFER/MOM/KAREN	Deborah Drakeford
MIKE/GLIB/TOM	Christopher Allen
JEFFREY/DOLLEY/PRODUCER/DAD/ROGER	Brian Dooley
JOGGER 3/AISHA/HARRIET TUBMAN/ COMRADE BLACK	Lucinda Davis
MARISSA/MISS SUE/ALICE	Chala Hunter

Director:	Micheline Chevrier
Associate Director:	Kwaku Okyere
Dramaturg:	Stephen Drover
Set Designer:	Jawon Kang
Costume Designer:	Nalo Soyini Bruce
Lighting Designer:	Michelle Ramsay
Sound Designer:	Thomas Ryder Payne
Assistant Sound Designer:	Samira Banihashemi
Videographer:	Frank Donato
Animator:	Dezmond Arnkvarn
Fight Director:	Jack Rennie
Stage Manager:	Daniel Oulton
Assistant Stage Manager:	Julian Smith
Rap Coach:	Donna-Michelle St. Bernard

CHARACTERS

WHAT KIND OF DOG IS THAT?

MARISSA: a white woman, thirty, married to Mike
MIKE: a Black man, late thirties, married to Marissa
JOHN: a Redbone coonhound, a dog, not a person, perhaps a puppet
CAMILLE: a white woman, forties, upper middle-class, John's owner, married to Jeffrey
JEFFREY: a white man, fifties, upper middle-class, John's owner, married to Camille
JOGGER 1: a Black man with a Caribbean accent
JOGGER 2: a white man
JOGGER 3: a Black woman
AISHA: a Black woman, thirties, Mike and Marissa's friend
JORDAN: a white man, thirties, Mike and Marissa's friend
GERALD: a Black man, thirties, dating Aisha

THE TRAIN HOME

GLIB: a Black man, thirties, runaway slave
DOLLEY: a white man, fifties, a Quaker, married to Jen
JENNIFER: a white woman, forties, a Quaker, married to Dolley
STILL: a Black man, thirties, bounty hunter
ZAC: a white man, thirties, bounty hunter
HARRIET TUBMAN: no explanation needed

NOW YOU TRY

MISS SUE: a young white girl, eight, think Shirley Temple
MR. JIMMY: a Black man, thirties, think Bojangles
PRODUCER: a white man, fifties

JAMAL MAKAMBE YATES IS COMING TO DINNER

MOM: a white woman, late forties, owner of a Tesla dealership, married to Dad

ALICE: a young white woman, twenties, studying social sciences at Howard

JAMAL: a white man, thirties, professor of English (focus on Tolkien) at Howard

DAD: a white man, fifties, doctor, Howard University enthusiast, married to Mom

THE BLACK AGENDA

COMRADE BLACK: a Black woman, thirties, ship's crew

COMRADE BLACKITY BLACK: a Black man, thirties, ship's crew

KAREN: a white woman, forties, slave aboard the ship

GARVEY: the ship's computer, a voiceover with a Siri-type voice and a West African accent

ROGER: a white man, fifties, reparations candidate

TOM: a Black man, forties, reparations candidate

PRODUCTION NOTES

This play unfolds in two time signatures: the first, What Kind of Dog Is That?, is a through line that takes place in the present day in Vancouver, BC; the second is a series of play provocations that travel through time and space, satirical meditations on the ideas presented by the through line.

For transitions between the time signatures, follow the dog. This prompt is open for creative interpretation.

An example of the "follow the dog" prompt – Jesse Lipscombe as Mike and Goose as John in *Redbone Coonhound*, 2022: set design by Kevin McAllister; costume design by CS Fergusson-Vaux; lighting design by Jonathan Kim (Chimerik 似不像); photo by Moonrider Productions for the Arts Club Theatre Company

A slash / indicates characters speaking over each other.

A dash – indicates an interruption.

Chala Hunter as Marissa and Christopher Allen as Mike in *Redbone Coonhound*, 2022: set design by Jawon Kang; costume design by Nalo Soyini Bruce; lighting design by Michelle Ramsay; photo by Cylla von Tiedemann

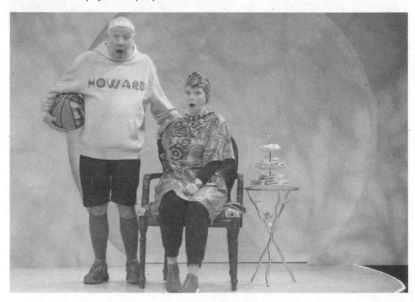

Brian Dooley as Dad and Deborah Drakeford as Mom in *Redbone Coonhound*, 2022: set design by Jawon Kang; costume design by Nalo Soyini Bruce; lighting design by Michelle Ramsay; photo by Cylla von Tiedemann

Emerjade Simms as Harriet Tubman in *Redbone Coonhound*, 2022: set design by Kevin McAllister; costume design by CS Fergusson-Vaux; lighting design by Jonathan Kim (Chimerik 似不像); photo by Moonrider Productions for the Arts Club Theatre Company

Emma Slipp as Miss Sue in *Redbone Coonhound*, 2022: set design by Kevin McAllister; costume design by CS Fergusson-Vaux; lighting design by Jonathan Kim (Chimerik 似不像); photo by Moonrider Productions for the Arts Club Theatre Company

Emerjade Simms as Comrade Black, Kwesi Ameyaw as Comrade Blackity Black, and Gerry Mackay as Roger in *Redbone Coonhound*, 2022: set design by Kevin McAllister; costume design by CS Fergusson-Vaux; lighting design by Jonathan Kim (Chimerik 似不像); photo by Moonrider Productions for the Arts Club Theatre Company

Christopher Allen as Glib in *Redbone Coonhound*, 2022: set design by Jawon Kang; costume design by Nalo Soyini Bruce; lighting design by Michelle Ramsay; photo by Cylla von Tiedemann

Gerry Mackay as Dad, Sebastien Archibald as Jamal, Emma Slipp as Alice, and Nancy Kerr as Mom in *Redbone Coonhound*, 2022: set design by Kevin McAllister; costume design by CS Fergusson-Vaux; lighting design by Jonathan Kim (Chimerik 似不像); photo by Moonrider Productions for the Arts Club Theatre Company

Jesse Lipscombe as Mike, Emerjade Simms as Aisha, Kwesi Ameyaw as Gerald, Sebastien Archibald as Jordan, and Emma Slipp as Marissa in *Redbone Coonhound*, 2022: set design by Kevin McAllister; costume design by CS Fergusson-Vaux; lighting design by Jonathan Kim (Chimerik 似不像); photo by Moonrider Productions for the Arts Club Theatre Company

REDBONE
COONHOUND

WHAT KIND OF DOG IS THAT?

PART 1

*English Bay, Vancouver. Sunny. Beautiful day for a run.
MIKE and MARISSA walk casually along the seawall. You
know, just having themselves a bit of a day. They attempt to
hold hands but their rhythm is off. It's awkward.*

MARISSA: Do you mind if we don't hold hands?

MIKE: Nope.

MIKE and MARISSA drop hands.

MARISSA: You just do this bobbing thing when you walk. You're
like a bouncy castle with legs.

MIKE: And you move like Baby Yoda.

MIKE spots something in the distance.

MIKE: Give me your hand back.

MARISSA: What? Why?

MIKE: That old speed-walking group.

MARISSA gives him a look.

MIKE: I want them to know that we're a couple, and I'm not, like,
sneaking up on you.

MIKE and MARISSA hold hands again.

MARISSA: I think someone should explain the concept of speed
walking to them. They're barely moving.

MIKE and MARISSA find a bench to sit on, drop hands again, and sit.

MARISSA: This is nice.

MIKE: Yeah. I've missed the one-legged crow skulking for scraps by the hotdog stand.

MIKE and MARISSA enjoy the view.

MARISSA: So how do you feel now that Black History Month is officially over?

MIKE: Good. I did it! I fixed all the racism!

MARISSA: (*feigning sincerity*) There's no more?

MIKE: Nope. I got it all.

MARISSA: That's good. Racism was bad. (*beat*) Any highlights from the tour you'd like to share?

MIKE: You know how after every school presentation I do a Q and A?

MARISSA: Oh no …

MIKE: Wait for it. An adorable little blond girl asked me, "Are you a slave?"

MARISSA: Dear God.

MIKE: Oh yeah. The kids busted out all the greatest hits this year.

MARISSA: "When's white history month?"

MIKE: "What about reverse racism?"

MARISSA: "Why can't I say the N-word?"

MIKE: Do you know the most popular answer to the question, "Who was the first Black person in Canada?"

MARISSA: Viola Desmond?

MIKE: Drake.

MARISSA: Well, he did start from the bottom and now he's here.

MIKE and MARISSA high-five.

MIKE: I honestly don't know if I can do it anymore.

MARISSA: Really?

MIKE: Yeah. I'm almost forty. Having to explain that Nicki Minaj is not the modern-day equivalent to Harriet Tubman or that the Underground Railroad was neither underground nor a railroad for the one-thousandth time is just ...

MARISSA: Exhausting?

MIKE: Yeah.

MARISSA: I get it. But you're home now. It's Saturday. It's a sort-of-beautiful day. We can just relax ...

CAMILLE and JEFFREY come into view finishing up the last lap of their morning jog. They begin to stretch and hydrate. Their dog JOHN exhibits loads of energy. He is not leashed.

MARISSA gasps.

MIKE: Jesus?! Why do you gasp so much?

MARISSA: Look at that dog. Look! Look! I have to say hi. I have to.

MIKE: Wait!

MARISSA moves towards CAMILLE and JEFFREY.

MIKE: (*to himself*) Annnnnd she's off.

MARISSA: Excuse me! Hi. Don't mean to bother you. Your dog. *Stunning.*

JEFFREY: It's no bother. We're in the cool-down phase of our run.

CAMILLE: Prestretch.

JEFFREY: But postrun.

CAMILLE: Twenty-six point two miles today.

JEFFREY: Not a PB.

CAMILLE: No, not a PB.

MARISSA: Mike, come say hi!

> *MIKE clearly doesn't want to join, but MARISSA loves dogs, so …*

MIKE: (*reluctantly*) Yeah. So great.

> *MIKE makes his way over.*

MARISSA: (*reaching out*) Can I pet him?

CAMILLE: He's a little aloof around new people.

JEFFREY: He may *bay.*

MIKE: (*nervously*) What's that? What's *bay*?

MARISSA: (*confidently*) Like a howl.

JEFFREY: No, he *bays.*

JOHN bays.

MIKE: FUCK! (*embarrassed*) Sorry. His bark is very ... robust.

JEFFREY: His bay. I think you mean bay.

MARISSA: Is he friendly? He looks friendly.

JEFFREY: Oh yes. Very friendly.

> *JOHN sees something, probably a little dog, and lunges or bays or jumps at the same time. He's Cujo all of a sudden. MIKE jumps out of the way as JOHN takes off up the hill.*

MIKE: WHOA!

JEFFREY: (*chuckling*) He just started doing that. (*beat*) John!

CAMILLE: Prey drive. Trait of the breed. (*beat*) John, come!

MIKE: Uh. Can he just be off leash like that?

JEFFREY: Oh yeah. (*beat*) John! Come! (*beat*) He'll come.

CAMILLE: He has very good recall.

MARISSA: He seems like a ... free spirit.

JEFFREY: Free spirit, yes, but also very trained. (*beat*)
   JOHN! JOHN!

CAMILLE: /JOHN!

JEFFREY: /JOHN!

CAMILLE: /JOHN!

JEFFREY: /JOHN!

CAMILLE: /JOHN!

JEFFREY: /JOHN!

CAMILLE: /JOHN!

JEFFREY: /JOHN!

JOHN comes back.

CAMILLE: See? There he comes.

JOHN goes right back to MIKE, sniffing him.

MIKE: (*laughing nervously*) He's getting right in the ol' crotch area, eh?

JEFFREY: Yes, he's playful.

CAMILLE: We wanted a dog that had a sense of humour.

JEFFREY: But also a guard dog.

MIKE: In Trinidad, they're all guard dogs.

JOGGER 1 runs by.

JOGGER 1: Beautiful dog! Just like mine back home!

MIKE: (*to himself*) The fuck ...

CAMILLE: Thank you!

JEFFREY: By the way, you're overstriding!

JOGGER 1: Go fuck your mother!

JEFFREY: Okay! Will do!

MARISSA: I love his name. John.

JEFFREY: Yup. John. Johnny-Johnny-John-John. Or Jo-Jo-Johnny-Ho-Ho. Sometimes I say that or JJ. J-wow. John, John, Jumpin' John who's the John? Who's the John?

CAMILLE: He's the John.

MARISSA: Awwww. Yeah. I'm going to try and pet him one more time.

> *MARISSA moves closer to JOHN.*

CAMILLE: Let him sniff you first. Let him do that and then if he wants to, he'll come to you.

MARISSA: Of course. I'll just be very still and see what happens. (*beat*) I love dogs.

> *JOHN ignores her and stays stuck on MIKE.*

JEFFREY: Look at that!

MIKE: Yup. Still just all over me!

JEFFREY: He loves you, doesn't he?

MIKE: Uh ... yeah, it's just that I don't really ... want that?

JEFFREY: He doesn't do that with just anybody.

MARISSA: I really love dogs. Does he ...? Maybe if I reach my hand out ...

> *MARISSA reaches her hand out close to JOHN's face. JOHN moves his head to the side, avoiding her.*

CAMILLE: Oh I think he has a fondness for the boys. Don't worry. He's not much of a cuddler with me either.

JEFFREY: Why do you ...?

CAMILLE: Why what?

JEFFREY: You're always implying that.

CAMILLE: What? What am I implying?

JEFFREY: Well, it's as if you're saying that our dog is *gay*, Camille.

CAMILLE: No, I'm not!

JEFFREY: You're always saying that about the cuddling. You're saying he's *gay*, Camille.

CAMILLE: No, I'm not, Jeffrey! He humps that stack of *Chatelaine* magazines in the bathroom. I tell people that all the time!

JEFFREY: That's still implying he's gay, Camille. It's *Chatelaine*!

MIKE: Sorry, could you grab him?

JEFFREY: What's the problem?

MIKE: He's just really *on me*.

    JOGGER 2 runs by.

JOGGER 2: Beautiful dog! What a specimen!

CAMILLE: Thank you!

    Pause.

JEFFREY: Why do you ...?

CAMILLE: What?/What now?

JEFFREY: /Why do you just jump in there like that?

CAMILLE: What do you mean jump?

JEFFREY: You always take the compliment before I have a chance to say anything.

CAMILLE: No, I don't! You got to take the compliment yesterday when that Asian couple said,/"He's a looker, isn't he?" YES, YOU DID.

JEFFREY: /No, no I didn't. YOU DID. You said, "He sure is!"

MARISSA attempts to distract JOHN away from MIKE.

MIKE: (*trying to leave again*) Maybe we should go ...?

MARISSA: (*quietly*) Right. (*to CAMILLE and JEFFREY*) Well, thanks for stopping.

JEFFREY: He's bred to run, you know?

CAMILLE: He's a tracker.

JEFFREY: Very scent driven.

MIKE: Can someone get this dog off of me ...?

JEFFREY: John!

There's no response from JOHN.

JOGGER 3 runs by.

JOGGER 3: Use a leash! Respect the bylaws!

JEFFREY: (*calling after her*) /He's TRAINED!

CAMILLE: (*calling after her*) /FASCIST!

MARISSA: We should get going, actually. But he's really, really great.

JEFFREY: And rare. We had him shipped from *Louisiana*, so.

JEFFREY makes a knowing face at MIKE.

MIKE: /... awesome.

MARISSA: /Oh, my husband's not American.

CAMILLE: /Snatched him right off his mama's tit. All his little brothers and sisters cried and cried!

JEFFREY imitates the moment.

JEFFREY: A-whoooooooooooo!

CAMILLE: Just like that. They went, "A-whooooo!!"

JOHN starts baying loudly.

MIKE: What kind of dog is that?

CAMILLE and JEFFREY: (*proudly*) *A Redbone coonhound!*

Pause.

MIKE: The fuck you just say?

THE TRAIN HOME

We follow the dog to ...

... a new world. Somewhere between Michigan and Mississippi, 1858. The sun sinks from its high place in the sky. Soon it will be dark. We hear distant howls.

GLIB hides in tall grass, breathless from running.

GLIB: (*breathing heavily*) Goddamn ... I think I finally shook those mutts.

As GLIB waits, the light of a lantern creeps closer and closer. Suddenly DOLLEY emerges. He's flanked by JENNIFER, who has many bags, pots, and pans tied to every part of her. She's a human wagon.

DOLLEY: (*calling from a distance*) Come along, Jennifer. Our coloured friends will be here by now!

JENNIFER: (*calling from a distance*) Coming!

GLIB: Shit. White people! Let me hide behind this forked tree that perfectly hides my body and purpose.

DOLLEY: Ah! The forked tree! This is the spot, Jennifer.

GLIB: Fuck.

DOLLEY: As I assume Moses would have wanted, I shall play my flute to signal that it is safe to emerge from wherever it is they may be hiding. (*beat*) Jennifer, hand me my wooden throng of song.

JENNIFER rummages through everything on her person.

DOLLEY: Jennifer, why isn't this immediate?

JENNIFER: I'm sorry, my love. I'm carrying everything you own on my back and front.

> *JENNIFER finds the flute.*

But here it is. Your flute.

DOLLEY: Ew. Don't touch the embouchure with your fingers. Handle up, Jennifer.

> *DOLLEY plays a wooden flute, emulating the twitter sounds a small bird would make.*

> *Flute twitter.*

> *Silence.*

> *Flute twitter.*

> *More silence. Then ...*

DOLLEY: (*whispering loudly*) Good morrow, weary travellers. No need to stay "underground."

> *GLIB stays deadly silent.*

JENNIFER: Reveal yourselves! Salvation awaits!

DOLLEY: (*to JENNIFER*) Jennifer ...?

JENNIFER: Oh. Sorry. "No talkies to the darkies."

DOLLEY: That's right. Good girl. (*back to GLIB*) Brethren? Your "conductor" is here.

> *GLIB emerges from his hiding place.*

GLIB: (*unsure*) Moses? Is that you?

DOLLEY: Ah! There you are! Hello, coloured friend! Congratulations on completing the first leg of your arduous journey, and looking quite well considering! You must be famished. We have figs and a full wheel of cheese. Standby as Jennifer serves us and gets on all fours to act as our table.

JENNIFER gets down on her hands and knees.

GLIB: Okay ... a bit of proto: (*standing in front of DOLLEY*) Who the fuck are *you*? (*looking down at JENNIFER*) Who the fuck are *you*? Can I have some cheese? And where the fuck is Moses?

DOLLEY cuts the wheel of cheese with a pocket knife and distributes it.

JENNIFER: I'M JENNIFER! WHO THE FUCK ARE YOU?

DOLLEY gives JENNIFER a warning look and shushes her.

GLIB: I'm Glib.

DOLLEY: (*slowly and loudly*) And I am Milhouse, of the Dolley Clan.

GLIB: Let me tell you something right now: I don't want nothing to do with no clans. So you better preach a different sermon.

DOLLEY: Of course! Preaching is what I do best! Our family, the Dolleys, are from a long line of Christians known as Protestants known as Quakers. We are a subset of a subset. We believe slavery is a vile practice: YUCK, YUCKY. These beliefs led us to join the resistance under Moses.

GLIB: Okay. Let me take another lap around this track. (*clapping his hands*) Where-the-fuck-is-Moses?

JENNIFER: You mean Harriet? I think she's in Philadelphia! On a secret mission!

DOLLEY: Jennifer! Away!

JENNIFER walks away. She tries to quiet the sound of pots and pans clanging loudly as she moves.

DOLLEY: Now, back to your question about Moses. We call her Mrs. Tubman. We've never met her, but she lives in legend all around us. She's in the trees. In that cheese. Do you feel it, brother?

GLIB: I'm no white man's brother, devil. But that do sound like a bad bitch.

DOLLEY: Yes, she is.

We hear the sound of trees rustling.

GLIB: Slavers! Hide!

DOLLEY: Unnecessary. We have a protocol for this.

GLIB: Tell me you brought guns?!

DOLLEY: No need. I was assigned this mission because I am trained in the art.

Pause.

GLIB: (*eagerly*) Of what?!

DOLLEY: Just art. (*proudly*) I am a thespian.

GLIB: A what-pian?

DOLLEY: I am certified in the art of mimicry. I have portrayed all of the major characters in the Good Book at our annual Q-fest jamboree.

> *A rough-looking slaver, ZAC, comes into view, flanked by a Black bounty hunter, STILL.*

GLIB: There's two of them coming.

> *The sound of pots and pans again.*

DOLLEY: They've got Jennifer. (*beat*) Fiddlesticks and Juniperglucks!

GLIB: She doesn't seem hurt ...

DOLLEY: You're right. She's linked arms and is laughing with the slaver's coloured accomplice. He's quite tall and commanding, isn't he?

GLIB: Look at that sellout, helping white men catch his brothers and sisters. (*beat*) But that coat, though ...

DOLLEY: Watch me dazzle these scamps.

> *DOLLEY adopts an outrageously bad or broad Southern accent.*

Evenin' partner!

GLIB: Oh hell nah ...

> *ZAC and STILL walk towards them.*

JENNIFER: (*in an equally if not more outrageous accent*) Darlin'. Look who found me, lost and delirious!

GLIB: We gon die.

JENNIFER: These fine gentlemen helped escort me back to our picnic spot!

DOLLEY: Much obliged, gentlemen. My wife wanders. She's a little ho-hum in the head drum.

ZAC: No trouble. No trouble at all. This here's my tracker, Still, and I'm Zacharius Southernwood. You here for the bounty on him? (*using the barrel of his gun to point at GLIB*)

DOLLEY: Name's Jebbediaus ... Southern ... stump, and I reckon you must be mistaken. This here ... *boy* belongs to me. So you can lower your rifle, sir.

ZAC: "Southernstump," did you say?

DOLLEY: That's right.

ZAC: Well, Mr. Southern*stump*, in the South, and every part of the South I've been to, and I've been to every part of the South, we keep our property in shackles when off the plantation, ain't that right, Still?

STILL: I've been down South with your wife plenty of times.

ZAC: (*unsure*) Oh ... my Clarabell must have subcontracted him without my knowledge ... but that's fine, right? ... That's fine ... it is a long journey, especially in the dark ...

STILL: *Very long. And very dark.*

    ZAC and DOLLEY are uncomfortable.

DOLLEY: Cheese anyone?

JENNIFER: We have figs, too!

    JENNIFER holds up a fig. STILL takes it and eats sensually while looking at ZAC.

STILL: I love the sweet juices of a soft, plump fig in my mouth.

JENNIFER: My, my ...

DOLLEY: Quite an appetite on your friend there ...

ZAC: Yes, well ... uh ... Still here bought his freedom. How come that one ain't shackled? You let your niggers run free?

DOLLEY: No, I don't let my ... nnn run –

ZAC: Your what?

DOLLEY: My what?

ZAC: Sorry, I didn't catch that. Your what?

DOLLEY: Yes. /My ... yes. Exactly.

ZAC: /Your what? What? WHAT?

GLIB: Excuse me, Mr. Enslaver. Can you give us a moment?

DOLLEY: Pardon me, gentlemen. I must have a word with my nnnn ...

ZAC: Your what?

DOLLEY: My nnnni ...

ZAC: Your WHAT?

  GLIB pulls DOLLEY away.

GLIB: (*hushed*) What's wrong with you?!

DOLLEY: (*hushed*) What are you doing? I've got him by the dingleberries.

GLIB: Say it! You have to say it!

DOLLEY: Absolutely not!

GLIB: They're going to kill us if you don't! You're being a shitty ally! Say the N-word!

DOLLEY: But you're not even saying it!

GLIB: I'm not gonna say it! I hate that word!

DOLLEY: Well, so do I!

GLIB: Not as much as me, you don't!

DOLLEY: I CANNOT!

GLIB: Just act! It's your character saying it, right? Not you!

DOLLEY: No, my Jebbediaus would not say that word.

GLIB: But ... you're playing a slaver. Slavers say the N-word.

DOLLEY: No! Jebediah Southernstump has a complicated backstory!

GLIB: Motherfucker, by not saying it you're romanticizing the barbarity of slavers!

ZAC: Yoo-hoo! Little hens over there cluckin' and buckin'. I can hear you! Cut the bullshit! We both know you ain't from around here, Jebbediaus *Southernstump*. Are you one of them saviour types ...?

ZAC spits.

ZAC: I've come across a few of you in my time and y'all seemed a few wheels short of a wagon.

GLIB: Don't do it ...

DOLLEY: As a matter of fact ...

GLIB: Lord have mercy, he's going to do it.

DOLLEY: (*deliberately breaking his accent*) ... I *AM* a few wheels short of a wagon! And your wagons would be lacking in wheels as well if you rolled off the beaten path, away from bigotry byway and on to compassion concourse!

> ZAC *spits again.*

ZAC: Still. Would you mind grabbing the runaway?

> STILL *grabs* GLIB.

GLIB: Get your greasy fig hands off of me!

ZAC: Listen here Mr. ... uh ...?

DOLLEY: (*proudly*) I am Milhouse Dolley. My homeland is a utopia where everyone is seen as equal.

JENNIFER: Not everyone!

DOLLEY: Our brown-skinned brethren are free to pursue any career their heart desires, from working outside in the sun –

JENNIFER: And snow and rain and hailstorms!

DOLLEY: – to working inside a benevolent white man's home.

GLIB: Wait. What?

DOLLEY: A treasure trove of domestic adventures!

GLIB: A treasure trove in the what now?

DOLLEY: I know! It sounds too good to be true! (*to Zac*) If you could just see that we are more alike than different.

We hear the sound of an approaching train.

GLIB: What the fuck? Is that a full-ass train? I thought the railroad was a metaphor?

DOLLEY: (*gasping*) Blessed assurance! Can it really be ...?

From a distance, HARRIET TUBMAN appears riding atop a locomotive.

HARRIET TUBMAN: CHOO-CHOO, MOTHERFUCKERS!

GLIB: It is! It's Harriet!

ZAC: Get out of the way, Still! That train's coming right at us!

STILL attempts to run but discovers that his coat is caught on a tree branch.

STILL: I can't! My opulent fur coat is stuck on this branch! Help me!

ZAC: (*struggling with the coat*) There. Got it. Oh. Son-of-a –

The train hits and kills ZAC and STILL.

GLIB: Holy shit! You motherfuckers just got Underground Railroaded!

An aggressive hip hop beat plays. They all look around, confused. HARRIET TUBMAN descends from the train. Her powerful voice is heard rapping over the beat.

HARRIET TUBMAN:
Batten down ya chariots, it's fuckin' Harriet
Tubman, the scariest, bitch y'all hilarious

Batten down ya chariots, it's fuckin' Harriet
Tubman, the scariest, bitch y'all hilarious

Freeing sons and daughters, leading whites to slaughter
Baddies call me Daddy 'cause I'm their fuckin' father
Moses comin' harder, icon and a martyr
Wading in the water like a muthafuckin' otter

Batten down ya chariots, it's fuckin' Harriet
Tubman, the scariest, bitch ya'll hilarious
Batten down ya chariots, it's fuckin' Harriet
Tubman, the scariest, bitch ya'll hilarious

Some call me a legend, some think I'm a myth
Shit gets really real when they can feel the hollow tips
My shotgun, beats your pop gun, underground till I drop one
You brought whips, I brought tips
This bad bitch don't give a single shit!

Batten down ya chariots, it's fuckin' Harriet
Tubman, the scariest, bitch y'all hilarious
Batten down ya chariots, it's fuckin' Harriet
Tubman, the scariest, bitch y'all hilarious

> The beat suddenly cuts out. HARRIET TUBMAN passes a
> shotgun to JENNIFER.

HARRIET TUBMAN: (*whispering*) Got a vision, clearly see 'em
Bad men are dead, now it's off to FREEEEEEEEEDOM!

DOLLEY: (*playing his flute and then rapping*) Batten down ya
chariots, it's fucking Harriet!

> JENNIFER shoots DOLLEY in the chest and passes the
> gun back to HARRIET TUBMAN as she ascends back
> onto the train.

GLIB: OH! Oh! OH! Jen! You killed your husband?!

JENNIFER: Yes. Harriet showed me that all bad men must die, Glib. Her angry yet rhythmic bars convinced me to liberate myself. From now on, I vow to live my life as a Black woman would. (*beat*) Except for the hard parts!

A train whistle sounds.

JENNIFER: Come, Glib. Harriet's badass chariot beckons us hence.

GLIB: Get it, girl.

JENNIFER: I will get it, dark man!

GLIB: Yes! Off to Canada where I can live the rest of my days free from racism! Oh, they gonna loooooooooooove me!

WHAT KIND OF DOG IS THAT?

PART 2

Mike and Marissa's condo in the West End of Vancouver. MIKE is at his laptop while MARISSA cleans up for company.

MIKE: They're too fucking comfortable.

MARISSA: Who is?

MIKE: White people.

MARISSA: I'm white and I'm not comfortable. I always feel like I have to shit.

MIKE: Present company excluded.

MARISSA: Right. (*beat*) Are you cleaning? Because I'm cleaning and you said you'd help.

MIKE: Yeah, I am.

> *MIKE looks at a sock on the coffee table and pushes it under the couch.*

MIKE: "Redbone coonhound." Really? Looking me straight in the eyes when they said it, too ... *Like, really? Really?*

MARISSA: Should they have not looked at you when they said it? I think that would have been weird.

MIKE: They shouldn't have said it at all.

MARISSA: Well, you did ask them. And it's not like they came up with it. They're not nineteenth-century Quaker folk.

MIKE: They chose it.

MARISSA: If a Dalmatian was called a honky cracker, I'd still want one.

MIKE: Disney would not have made *One Hundred and One Honky Crackers* ...

MARISSA: Babe. (*beat*) You've got to eventually let it go. It's just some old-timey name that's not connected to what you think. (*beat*) You should have some fruit. You want some fruit?

MIKE: Like Adolf? Would you name your kid Adolf?

MARISSA: Absolutely not.

MIKE: Why? It's an old-timey name that's not connected to what you think.

MARISSA: Because I don't like the sound of it. Just like I don't like the sound of the name Jessica.

MIKE: If you met a kid named Adolf, you wouldn't be suspicious?

MARISSA: Of what? The threat of genocide?

MIKE: Well, I don't have that luxury.

MARISSA: Here we go ...

MIKE: You get to stroll through the world, just oblivious. Skipping down Right This Way, Ma'am, Lane.

MARISSA: Oh, I love that lane! That's the same lane where I get asked for blow jobs every morning from that guy in the camel-hair coat. Super safe. Super fun. Super great for me.

MIKE: White people think they're entitled to all the things.

MARISSA: Your wife is white people.

MIKE: Present company excluded.

MARISSA: I'm going to cut up some cantaloupe.
Do you want some?

MIKE: Is it cantaloupe or is it honeydew?

MARISSA: /It's cantaloupe.

MIKE: /Because I don't think you know the difference.

MARISSA: Oh my God, I know the difference! Is your blood sugar low? Because you're getting a little ...

MIKE: What?

MARISSA: Fucking annoying.

MARISSA goes into the kitchen to cut a cantaloupe.

MIKE: There are lots of other names. We don't need to defend the ones that have been tainted. Use Aaron, Austin, Albernathy.

MARISSA: (*from off*) We should probably add Ted to the cancelled list. Ted Bundy, you know. And Vladimir. John of John Wayne Gacy. And Donald. But then there's Donald Duck, so do they cancel each other out?

MIKE: Notice how those are all white guys?

MARISSA: I think there's a duck in there, actually.

MIKE: A white duck.

MARISSA comes out with a bowl of cut-up cantaloupe.

MARISSA: You're right. There are no shitty Black people. Oh wait. Bill Cosby. O.J. Simpson. New Kanye. Definitely R. Kelly. Michael Vick.

MIKE: You *would* say Michael Vick.

MARISSA: You would *defend* Michael Vick.

MIKE: Yeah. He messed with dogs. He did his time and now he's a dog activist.

MARISSA: That's literally the plot of *102 Dalmatians*. And now we've come full circle.

MIKE: (*warning*) This is peak ...

MARISSA: Don't.

MIKE: I'm just saying.

MARISSA: You're *just* about to piss me off.

MIKE: Well, you're doing it.

MARISSA: Don't.

> Pause. The threat hangs in the air.

MIKE: This is white feminism.

MARISSA: YOU JUST COULDN'T HELP YOURSELF.

MIKE: You're right. I call it like I see it. You have moments. And this is a moment.

MARISSA: So loving dogs is white feminism?

MIKE: Loving dogs over Black men is.

MARISSA: I don't love anybody or anything over anything or anybody. I just don't give a fuck about a guy who mutilated and tortured dogs. He can fuck off with his cynical activism.

MIKE: He DID. He fucked off to prison for eighteen months. George Zimmerman got less time for MURDER.

MARISSA: Why are you still bringing up George Zimmerman as a counter? As if anyone here thinks he's a swell guy. (*beat*) Also, let's not forget about dear Georgie's domestic incident.

MIKE: You WOULD care about that more than, you know ... / THE BLACK CHILD MURDERING!

MARISSA: /IN ADDITION TO. God, you're always ... like ... you don't care about the shit these people do to women.

MIKE: Okay.

MARISSA: It's true! Unless it's racially motivated, you're the forgiving tree – just handing out passes. (*beat*) Like the NFL. Girlfriend punchings, wife beatings, wife murders – that's all excusable. I had to navigate rape-apologist conversations about Ben Roethlisberger with your high school friends – nay, not just navigate – but watch them eat my chips and dip while they did it in front of me like I didn't exist. But when Colin Kaepernick knelt down during the anthem and the backlash started? BOOM. Solidarity. No more football. No more chips and dip.

MIKE: Colin Kaepernick was in addition to all the other stuff.

MARISSA: Have you read that one *New York Times* article I sent you on endometriosis?

MIKE: I already know about your endo.

MARISSA: Aisha and I had a forty-five minute conversation about my ovarian cysts and her grapefruit-sized fibroids and your contribution was, "Oh no. That sucks" and then you went back to playing Wordle.

MIKE: Again. I already know about your endo.

MARISSA: Oh yeah? What do you know about it?

MIKE: I know it makes you moody.

MARISSA: You're right. The stabbing, debilitating pain in my sides that has required multiple surgeries makes me moody. What's your excuse? Not enough carbs?

MIKE: I'm not in the headspace for this. Truly.

MARISSA: Look, I'm not saying I know anything about being Black, but you dismiss all the things related to my womanhood as being way less important.

MIKE: No, I don't.

MARISSA: You call me a bitch when we're fighting.

MIKE: I don't call YOU a bitch. Sometimes Black people just say "bitch" at the beginning of a sentence. Like, "Bitch, I wish you would yell at me again for leaving socks on the floor." It's the universal bitch. Not the accusatory one.

MARISSA: Why does it feel like we have to rank oppression to get equal airtime? We're supposed to be each other's lighthouses in this sea of ... muck.

MIKE: It's not about ranking. It's completely different. If you made an accusation against me, you would be believed over me. End of story.

MARISSA: Is this like a deep-seated fear you have? Why do you think that I would *ever* put you in a position where I would be believed over you? About anything. That's truly horrifying. That you think that way.

MIKE: Because all white people are capable of doing this.

MARISSA: In the context of our marriage, I can't be all white people. I'm not the farmer's market. And why are you talking as if the justice system is uniquely unfair to you? This is exactly what I'm saying. I know it's not about ranking, but race does take precedence in our marriage.

MIKE: Good.

MARISSA: Every time?

MIKE types furiously on his laptop.

MARISSA: Hello?

MIKE: What? No. Not every time.

MARISSA: That's all I'm saying. (*beat*) What are you doing? Eat your fruit.

MIKE: Never mind what I'm – A-HA! Descendant of foxhounds, possibly Irish hounds, and *bloodhounds*. (*beat*) Bloodhounds. "The bloodiest threat to runaway slaves." The motherfuckers that made Harriet Tubman wade in the water.

MARISSA: OH MY GOD. It wasn't a bloodhound.

MIKE: No, it was a Redbone coonhound. Worse. How does one dog name have TWO racial slurs in it?

MARISSA: Truthfully, I didn't even know that "redbone" was a dig at light-skinned Black people.

MIKE: Not many people know any of this shit. The programming is real. Look at your family. You still watch Shirley Temple movies.

MARISSA: We put those on for my nonna. Christ. She's ninety-five years old. She's practically survived two World Wars. What am I going to do? Tell her she can't watch the TCM network?

MIKE: "Coon" is the worst one.

MARISSA: Come on! Worse than the N-word?

MIKE: Yes, if a Black person calls another Black person that, it's worse.

MARISSA: Really?

MIKE: Yes! It means you're a sellout. I can't believe I have to teach this in my own home. I used to get called a coon because I was a good student. It's disgusting.

MARISSA: I agree, babe. But I don't think Redbone coonhound is all of that! It's a dog breed. It's just a dog name you're putting all of this stuff on top of. It's not as deep as you're making it.

MIKE: Of course it's as deep as I'm making it. What are you saying?

MARISSA: Why don't you let this go?

MIKE: Because it hurts me! It hurts me to hear it, it hurts me to think about it, it hurts me to even say it to you, to have to explain it to you, to my wife, my white wife who will be the mother to my Black children. Would you want your child to be called a sellout? Two nickels always short. Shucking and jiving, wide teeth-grinning, watermelon-eating, chicken-stealing, inarticulate, buffoon? A red-lipped, tar-skinned, dumb, tap-dancing, cotton-picking, self-hating, white wife–marrying – a subhuman sambo. I HATE IT. IT HURTS TO

HEAR IT SAID, IT HURTS TO SAY IT, IT HURTS TO HAVE BEEN CALLED IT, AND WHITE PEOPLE HAVE NO RIGHT USING IT CASUALLY FOR SOMETHING AS ARBITRARY AS A FUCKING DOG-BREED NAME!

NOW YOU TRY

We follow the dog to ...

... a soundstage in Hollywood, 1935. Long red-velvet curtains are drawn. In the centre, a spotlight illuminates the text: The Miss Sue Show!

VOICEOVER: Live from Twentieth Century-Fox's lot in sunny Los Angeles, California, it's *The Miss Sue Show*! Starring the suave and singular singing sensation of 1935, little Miss Susie Shriner – star of hit films *Little Missy Mop Top*, *Sassy L'il Showgirl*, and *Bouncing Baby Boop Boop*. Today's episode features the co-star of her upcoming film, *Bongo Pongo in the Congo*, the sensational Jimmy Jingles Jameson! Ladies and gentlemen, please give a warm welcome to: Miss Sue!

The curtains part to reveal a stage adorned with a large, beautiful staircase in the foyer of a mansion.

MR. JIMMY stands dutifully by the bottom of the staircase, looking up at MISS SUE, who happily trots down.

MISS SUE: Mr. Jimmy, I've got a lot to say: BOOP, BOOP, DEE-DAW, DEE-DAW!

We hear an audience laugh track.

MR. JIMMY: Was that it?

MISS SUE: No!

MR. JIMMY: Well, you best say it, Miss Sue!

MISS SUE: Aw, shucks!

MR. JIMMY: What's wrong, Miss Sue?

MISS SUE: I forgot what it was I was gonna say!

We hear more audience laugh track.

MR. JIMMY: You know what helps me to remember things?

MISS SUE: Shaking your head like this? (*shaking her head back and forth violently*) Duh-ya-ya-ya-ya!

More audience laugh track.

MR. JIMMY: No, Miss Sue! I dance this here dance.

MR. JIMMY erupts into a classic tap dance. He moves gracefully up and down the lush staircase, making kazoo sounds with his mouth.

MISS SUE watches, lying down on her belly, resting her chin on her fists, big eyes ablaze.

MR. JIMMY: I went to the Safeway.

ALL: DEE-DAW, DEE-DAW!

MR. JIMMY: To get me some beef.

ALL: DEE-DAW, DEE-DAW!

MR. JIMMY: It was down by the laneway.

ALL: DEE-DAW, DEE-DAW!

MR. JIMMY: Had to move my feet!

ALL: DEE-DAW, DEE-DAW!

MR. JIMMY finishes his dance with a little TA-DA! flourish.

MISS SUE: Geez Louise! You sure can dance, Mr. Jimmy!

MR. JIMMY: All likeable negroes can dance, Miss Sue!

We hear applause.

MISS SUE: Yeah, sure, but how did you get to be so good?

MR. JIMMY: Well, I could show you, but it ain't easy being me. You wanna try?

MISS SUE: Uh-huh! I sure do wanna be like *you*, Mr. Jimmy!

MISS SUE goes offstage to get a can of tar and a roller.

MISS SUE: First, I'll paint myself black with this roller and some tar!

We hear the audience say, "awwwww."

MR. JIMMY: That's not what I mean, Miss Sue!

MISS SUE: Well, what do you mean, then?

MR. JIMMY: Take hold of my hand.

MISS SUE: Okay!

MR. JIMMY: First take these shoes and put 'em on quick, filled with tiny needles and made of brick!

MR. JIMMY hands MISS SUE a pair of shoes that look identical to his.

MR. JIMMY: If you wanna walk the walk, you gotta pay the levy.

MISS SUE goes to put them on.

MISS SUE: WOW-EEE. These sure are heavy!

MR. JIMMY: First put on the left one, then the right.

MISS SUE: (*laughing nervously*) I regret inquiring about your plight!

MR. JIMMY: Float up those stairs light as a cloud.

MISS SUE struggles up the stairs.

MISS SUE: My dogs are barkin' really loud!

MR. JIMMY: Hold this boulder and then you're done!

MR. JIMMY gives MISS SUE a boulder.

MISS SUE: (*holding the boulder*) Geez Louise! This weighs a ton!

MR. JIMMY: Ready? Set? Here we go! The last step is –

MISS SUE trips down the staircase.

MR. JIMMY: – look out below!

MISS SUE lands at the bottom with a loud thud.

MISS SUE: Wowie owie! I fell down the stairs!

MR. JIMMY: Yup! I bet that hurt!

MISS SUE: The blood is creeping down my skirt!

MR. JIMMY: Ooooh, it's totally soaked!

MISS SUE: I really think my leg is broke!

MR. JIMMY: Looks like both of those ankles, too!

MISS SUE: Golly gosh, that might be true! I really would like this to stop ...

MR. JIMMY: That's too bad kid, *boppity bop!*

MR. JIMMY does a little tap dance, then points at MISS SUE.

MR. JIMMY: You've seen my moves, now you try!

The lights slowly start to fade around MISS SUE as she tries to get up.

MR. JIMMY leaves.

ALL: DEE-DAW, DEE-DAW!

MISS SUE: Ow!

ALL: DEE-DAW, DEE-DAW!

MISS SUE: No, seriously, it really hurts!

ALL: DEE-DAW, DEE-DAW!

We hear the audience laugh track. PRODUCER enters.

PRODUCER: Cut! (*beat*) Hey boy, reset the props.

MR. JIMMY comes back to clear the set.

PRODUCER: Thanks, everybody. Let's take ten. (*beat*) Great take Miss Sue! You're a GENIUS! Next time, could you try falling in the splits and give the audience a little peekaboo rowdy-roo?

MISS SUE: Okay.

PRODUCER: Bingo bongo, little Pongo. Oh, and instead of crying like you're doing now, why don't you try not crying?

MISS SUE: Okay.

PRODUCER: This is why you're a pro, Miss Sue-Baloo. When we're done, I've got five close friends who want to meet you at Hotel No Tell.

MISS SUE: Again?

PRODUCER: Yup! Tomorrow night, too! Whap-whap-a-doo!

The lights fade.

WHAT KIND OF DOG IS THAT?

PART 3

Mike and Marissa's condo. MIKE and AISHA hang out in the living room. AISHA sorts through the magazines laid out on the coffee table, disappointed in Mike's selections.

AISHA: *SLAM* magazine? What are you? Twelve?

MIKE: It's on auto-renewal.

AISHA: For twenty-five years? And what's this shit? An *Oprah* magazine? Really?

MIKE: That's Marissa's.

AISHA: Damn. It's true: all white women need is Black Oprah, white wine, and scented candles.

MIKE: How did these people rule us for three hundred years?

AISHA: Bruh, Canada's only, like, a hundred and fifty years old.

MIKE: I wasn't just talking about Canada, I was talking about the US.

AISHA: Right.

MIKE: Ph.Ds. That's what we have in white people-ology. You'd think they would have taken at least *one* freshman course on the Black experience.

AISHA: At SFU, I could have sworn we used to say "first year." Now it's "freshman"?

MIKE: Same difference.

AISHA: You're obsessed. *Obsessed* with America.

MIKE: I'm obsessed with Black liberation.

AISHA: Says the guy who never dated a Black woman. (*beat*) Actually, you dated girls who were antithetical to Black women.

MIKE: What does that even mean?

AISHA: All of your ex-girlfriends looked like birds.

MIKE: "Birds?"

AISHA: Yes. And not crows or ravens either. Egrets, cranes, herons, swans. The sisters at the Black student union nicknamed you Orn.

MIKE: Bunch of woketivist feminists making O.J. Simpson jokes. Classy ...

AISHA: (*laughing*) That wasn't an O.J. joke. We called you Orn because it was short for ornithologist. 'Cause of all the white bird-ladies you dated.

AISHA laughs hysterically, miming binoculars.

MIKE: (*sarcastically*) It's so weird that I never dated Black women.

AISHA: And it's so weird that I've never dated white men.

MIKE: Listen, Black people make up 3 percent of Canada's population. Some of us have to stack the odds in our favour.

AISHA: The odds of you not marrying a Caucasoid were always slim to nil.

MIKE: I could barely find a Black woman to ask for directions let alone date and fall in love with.

Pause.

AISHA: You could have dated me.

MIKE: Really?

AISHA: Ew. No. You're like Canada's Carlton Banks.

MIKE: And there it is right there! You sisters are always talking about how Black men don't want to date you, but unless a brotha was Tupac, you weren't trying to date us.

AISHA: Excuse me? My man is the opposite of Tupac.

MIKE: Your current man would arrest all of the Pac prototypes you dated in college.

AISHA: That was the swag back then, okay? You just never had any drip.

MIKE: I was plenty ... drippy ...

AISHA: Hey, you made your marital nest, Orn. Now get comfy.

MIKE: I am comfy, and let the record show, Marissa is no bird.

AISHA: (*conceding*) That she is not. She is cool people.

MIKE: Most of the time.

AISHA: Oh no. Okay. What happened?

MIKE: We ran into this couple and their dog.

AISHA: Uh-oh. Did you scream again?

MIKE: A little bit, but this thing was all up in my shit!

AISHA: People expect you to like their dog as much as they do.

MIKE: Right?

AISHA: But I don't. I don't like your dog as much as you do.
I don't know your dog. I've never seen your dog before
in my life.

MIKE: That's all I'm saying.

AISHA: I saw this woman who couldn't have been more than
ninety pounds after a full meal, and she was walking a
literal wolf.

MIKE: Say word.

AISHA: No, I swear. I asked her. Point-blank. A timber wolf,
she says, like the craziest shit ever didn't just come out of her
mouth. She's got *Game of Thrones* tied to a string, hanging off
her bony wrist. What's she gonna do? That thing decides to
channel the spirit of his canine ancestors and come after me?
What's she gonna do?

MIKE: Nothing. This is the same thing that couple pulled with me.
Their dog was on me like a steak dinner. And then didn't they
casually tell me the fucker's breed was a Redbone coonhound –

AISHA: A what now?

MIKE: A RED-BONE COON-HOUND.

AISHA: Lord have mercy. White people have been doing the most.

MARISSA and JORDAN arrive out of earshot.

MARISSA: Redbone coonhound.

JORDAN: Oh no way. *Where the Red Fern Grows*! That was
the first book that ever made me cry. Those dogs are sick.
My cousin had one.

MARISSA: Whatever you do: don't mention that.

JORDAN: Why not?

MARISSA: I told you. Mike is sensitive about it. With good reason, obviously.

JORDAN: Because Mike hates dogs?

MARISSA: He doesn't hate them, and no. That's not why. It's the name. It's loaded. Think about it from his perspective.

Pause.

Redbone. Coon.

Pause.

They're racial slurs towards Black people.

JORDAN: No, they're not!

MARISSA: Yes, they are!

JORDAN: Okay, yes, maybe, as words, independently. But those dogs were bred to chase raccoons up trees. RA-coon. The Redbone thing, I don't know what that is. Maybe because of their fur colour?

MARISSA: No, actually, I looked it up and an early breeder of the dog was a man named Peter Redbone. But that's not ... look, the origin of the words doesn't matter. It's the impact today. Just ... don't bring it up around Mike.

JORDAN: What are we doing? Mike's my boy. Since when do I need coaching to be around him?

MARISSA: 2016? Around there? (*beat*) Also, you can't call a Black man "boy," *kiddo.*

JORDAN: This is gonna be fun ...

MARISSA and JORDAN enter the condo.

MARISSA: Hey! We're back!

JORDAN: We've got drinks!

AISHA: Finally!

MARISSA: Sorry. I feel like we were gone for a long time.

> *MARISSA and JORDAN put down a selection of*
> *international drinks, including White Claws for MIKE and*
> *Erdinger non-alcoholic beer for JORDAN.*

JORDAN: Aisha! Hey girl! What's up?

AISHA: Hey Jo-Jo.

> *AISHA and JORDAN high-five. JORDAN offers his*
> *hip for a bump.*

AISHA: No.

JORDAN: You used to do it.

AISHA: I did it once when we first met fifteen years ago, and I've
regretted it ever since.

JORDAN: You regret meeting me or hip bumping me?

AISHA: Both. Obviously.

MARISSA: Aw, it's just like old Friday night pub crawls.

> *MARISSA kisses MIKE on the cheek.*

JORDAN: Minus the puking.

AISHA: On my new Jordans, Jordan.

JORDAN: (*to Aisha and Mike*) I thought for sure you two were dating.

AISHA: /Of course you did.

MIKE: /Shocking.

JORDAN: No, not because of that. Because of the way Mike jumped up to save those shoes.

MIKE: The spirit of His Airness compelled me!

> *A little moment of levity ensues as MIKE mimes dunking, his body deliberately mimicking the iconic "Jump Man" logo made famous by Jordan Brand shoes and clothing.*

JORDAN: Yo Mike, did you think about the condo I was telling you about?

MARISSA: This again?

MIKE: Yeah man, we can't do that.

AISHA: What can't you do?

MIKE: Jordan wants us to go in on some presale condo deal in Victoria.

JORDAN: I want to set you guys up. The last one I bought went up, like, 30 percent.

MARISSA: Housing is a human right, not a fucking investment opportunity.

JORDAN: Suit yourself, but real estate changed my life. And I want my friends to win.

AISHA: Didn't you just buy a million-dollar house?

MIKE: Two point three million.

JORDAN: And it's worth two point six now. I got a deal. The previous owners had to sell it fast.

MARISSA: And tell everyone why, Jordan.

JORDAN: (*excitedly*) The couple got divorced. Wanted to split their assets quick.

AISHA: Woooooow ...

JORDAN: Hey, I don't make the rules. I just play the cards I'm dealt.

MARISSA: And if you don't like the cards you're dealt, you just go to a rich friend and borrow the money for a down payment.

JORDAN: There's no shame in leveraging your network.

MIKE: Totally agree. Hey Jordan, can we borrow two hundred grand?

JORDAN: Can't. I still have to pay back the money I borrowed for my rental property.

AISHA: In what bloodclaat world is Jordan a landlord while the rest of us are out here renting?

JORDAN: It's a world we can all live in together. Just sayin'.

MIKE: Okay, pass me a White Claw, RE/MAX.

> *JORDAN passes MIKE a White Claw.*

JORDAN: I almost got you the watermelon. *Almost.*

MIKE: Dude.

JORDAN: I said almost!

MIKE: It's a principle issue.

JORDAN: I know.

MIKE: Same reason I won't eat fried chicken, at least not in public.

ALL: We know!

AISHA: For the record, I will eat both of those things publicly, privately, and proactively.

JORDAN: Uh, hells yeah.

> JORDAN *takes a non-alcoholic beer.*

JORDAN: Who wants to see me open this with my teeth?

MARISSA: /No thanks.

MIKE: /Nah.

AISHA: Dude. Why?

JORDAN: I don't know. It's just this awesome thing I learned how to do.

AISHA: Jordan, a supernova is awesome. Opening a beer with your dirty-ass teeth is disgusting.

> JORDAN *shrugs and opens his drink the normal way.*

MARISSA: Should we get Gerald?

AISHA: Yeah! Where is that fine-ass man of mine? One more unanswered text and I'm going to start taking things away that he likes, sexually.

JORDAN: Uh-oh! Someone's – gonna get it!

AISHA: No.

JORDAN: K.

MARISSA: Gerald's outside. He's been on the phone.

AISHA: With who?

MARISSA: I don't know. But I overheard him say "wide receivers" when we were coming in.

AISHA: Oh God. Stupid-ass fantasy-football draft.

MARISSA: Football season is like a cockroach: it never dies.

AISHA: Listen. Gerald's going to call his friend by this weird, super alpha-bro, sixteen-year-old nickname.

GERALD: (*offstage*) Okay, Smoke Star! Talk to you later.

JORDAN: Smoke Star. That's pretty sick, actually.

AISHA: Settle down, Century 21 ...

JORDAN: Oh! BOOM! Roasted! Nice one, Eesh!

AISHA: No.

JORDAN: K.

> GERALD *enters the living room.*

GERALD: Hey, sorry I'm late. An old buddy called right as I was coming in.

AISHA: I guess not picking up wasn't an option?

GERALD: Glad to hear I'm not missing this sermon.

AISHA: Someone's looking to meet God tonight.

GERALD: Sorry, baby. It was a trade offer in my fantasy league.

MIKE: Vancouver's finest hard at work!

GERALD: Well, sports talk helps me unwind from a long day of being an ACTUAL justice warrior.

MIKE: "Warrior?" Is that what they're calling writing traffic tickets after hockey games now? Robson Street isn't exactly Sparta.

GERALD: And debating at dinner parties ain't exactly the Freedom March.

MARISSA: Interrupting this sparring session with a boring question: (*holding up drinks*) what country do you want to start with, G?

AISHA: Heads up, Mike's staying domestic tonight.

JORDAN: No laws when you're drinking Claws, eh, Mike?

JORDAN gives MIKE a hip bump. MIKE softly returns it.

GERALD: I literally just gave a warning to some high school girls for drinking those in a park.

MIKE: Well, they're refreshing. They're sugar-free. And I don't care if ya'll think I'm a pussy for drinking them.

AISHA: Can you not use that word as a slur?

MARISSA: Oh, Mike doesn't care about misogyny. He only cares about racism.

AISHA: And only towards Black men. Brothas have a way of making it about them.

MIKE: I mean, this conversation is literally about me, so.

MARISSA: A lot is literally about you.

MIKE: (*to Marissa*) Excuse me. This is Black business.

ALL react playfully.

MARISSA: Our whole marriage is Black business. I'm just a guest here, doling out the chips.

GERALD: Oh, is this another "Black"-only event?

MIKE: Yeah, man. My own wife wants to keep me in the Sunken Place.

MARISSA: Okay. The Sunken Place? Relax.

JORDAN: *Get Out.* Right? That reference?

MIKE: Yeah.

JORDAN: Cool. That film is so great. And you know, interesting how *Get Out* and *Othello* –

AISHA: We're not doing that right now, Jordan.

MIKE: Yeah, it was just a throwaway line, you know?

JORDAN: Oh. Yeah. No. For sure.

GERALD: Jesus, Aisha. Let the man talk about *Othello* if he wants to.

MARISSA: Seriously. Are we gatekeeping Shakespeare now?

AISHA: I'm not gatekeeping. You can have his frilly ass.

GERALD: See, Jordan, the cool thing these days is cancelling opinions you don't like. Very progressive.

AISHA: Some opinions are best left unsaid. And I'm not talking about making some safe space, woketivist echo chamber, so don't anybody give me a face.

MIKE: "Woketivist?" I'd settle on semi-conscious ...

MARISSA: Oh, is that in reference to me?

MIKE: Getting defensive, are we?

JORDAN: It's probably about me.

AISHA: No. No. Marissa, it's not about you.

JORDAN: See? It's about me.

AISHA: (*continuing*) No, Jordan. It's *definitely not* about you. Just when you think Black men are the most trifling, white dudes be like, "hold my Molson Ex."

JORDAN: I'm actually drinking an Erdinger currently – non-alcoholic – so (*physical gesture*) your stereotype.

GERALD: Hey, Dinger's the shit. Good call.

JORDAN: Also, I'm "white dudes" now? Cool.

AISHA: You've BEEN white dudes, Jordan. Your Instagram looks like *The Joe Rogan Experience*.

JORDAN: This again ... I listen to Joe Rogan for the GUESTS. He has interesting people on, and Mike listens to him, too.

MARISSA and AISHA give MIKE a look.

MIKE: What? He has interesting people on!

MARISSA: OH GOD.

AISHA: Really, Mike, because Don Cherry had "interesting guests" and you stopped watching him because racism.

MARISSA: But of course, Aisha. That whole thing fits perfectly within what directly affects Mike.

MIKE: First of all, Don Cherry definitely did not have interesting guests.

GERALD: Yeah, I don't think brothers are running to "Coach's Corner" for the hot takes.

JORDAN: Whoa, wait, backup. Joe Rogan is not a racist.

GERALD: /No, he's not.

MIKE: /No, he's not.

MARISSA: No, him and his dude bros just casually hate women. No big deal though, right?

MIKE: /Yes, okay, fine.

GERALD: /That's fair.

AISHA: This doesn't even register for Jordan. Look at his face.

JORDAN: Hey, whoa, I'm thinking. I'm not a jackhammer of opinions like you guys. And how come every time a conversation about race comes up, I stop being Jordan and turn into a punching bag?

AISHA: We're doing you a service. You're lucky you have a group of Black friends to keep your ass in check. Stop casting yourself as Hard Luck Harry.

JORDAN: (*laughing*) We all know who Hard Luck Harry is at this party.

No one knows.

AISHA: You gonna tell us?

JORDAN: Never mind.

MIKE: No, no, no. Please ...

JORDAN: Look, I'm sorry. Okay? Marissa told me that Mike is in a really sensitive place, and to not racially trigger him, and I –

AISHA: /Hold up. "Racially trigger ..."

MIKE: /Excuse me?

MARISSA: What? I just told him about what happened.

GERALD: What happened?

AISHA: Mike met these white people with a Redbone coonhound.

GERALD: A what?

MARISSA: I just said that you're a bit raw and to ... tread lightly.

MIKE: Tread lightly how?

GERALD: Hold up. A *what*?

ALL: A REDBONE COONHOUND.

MARISSA: (*continuing*) I told him not to be an idiot saying unintentionally dumb, insensitive, embarrassing shit.

JORDAN: Wow. Tell me how you really feel.

GERALD: Wait, why are you all saying Redbone coonhound like I'm supposed to know what that is?

JORDAN: It's a dog. My cousin had one.

MARISSA gives JORDAN a look.

MIKE: Oh, your cousin had one, did he?

JORDAN: /She.

AISHA: /Of course his cousin had one.

MARISSA: /I told you!

JORDAN: Yeah, she had a bluetick coonhound first and then she got a Redbone the next summer. (*beat*) What? She hunts! She's not going to get a shih tzu.

MIKE: Good to know the breed is alive and well in farm country.

MARISSA: It's not the dog's fault it exists and is doing what humans force it to do.

MIKE: Only a Karen would believe that.

JORDAN: /It's true!

MARISSA: /Oh piss right off.

AISHA: Mike, she's not a Karen. You wouldn't have married that kind of white lady.

MARISSA: If I'm a Karen, Mike's a mid-Kardashian Kanye.

AISHA: (*leaning in*) Ohhhh I need some snacks ...

MIKE: You mean an entrepreneurial, fashion-forward creative genius? Thank you.

MARISSA: Oh you're fashion-forward all right. Mike told me it was okay to buy a purse from that Coach-Basquiat collab!

AISHA: What the fuck is wrong with you, Mike? Letting your white wife make such a purchase.

MIKE: So we're going to pretend like Basquiat didn't LOVE white people? He was boys with Warhol and Bowie, the two whitest white guys ever.

AISHA: Basquiat was cool as shit. He could do whatever he wanted. But I don't fuck with corporations vulturing our culture.

JORDAN: Vulturing? Culture should be appreciated and shared.

MARISSA: I'm with Jordan. We've gotten it into our heads that we're supposed to re-segregate culture into these little silos, but that's actually counter to what culture means and what it is.

JORDAN: You don't see Marissa's nonna getting mad at the world for chowing down on lasagna.

MARISSA: No, she's mad at the world for eating *frozen* lasagna – as if that's real Italian food ...

AISHA: It's not the same thing.

GERALD: Why not?

AISHA: Why not? Because one is lasagna and one is bloodclaat Babylon thieving from we.

MIKE: (*to Marissa*) If you like the purse, keep the purse.

MARISSA: I just like that it has a dinosaur on it!

GERALD: Listen, this appropriation stuff is a western-ass idea. If Jordan came to Nigeria –

JORDAN: Which I plan to. Stoked.

GERALD: – my family would be honoured if he wore traditional garb. It would be seen as a compliment.

MIKE: Yes, but that's coming from a very generous place. The west made it a problem, like they always do, by commodifying everything.

MARISSA: So allyship is about intention?

JORDAN: 'Cause I intend to rock a dashiki when I'm in Abuja.

AISHA: You're gonna look like one of those pasty missionaries with African prints draped over your flat ass ...

ALL laugh, except for JORDAN.

AISHA: (*to Jordan, teasing*) What's up with you?

MIKE: Let's take a break from dunking on Jordan.

JORDAN: No, it's nothing. Dunk away.

AISHA: So what, then?

JORDAN: I was just thinking about how you guys taught me that everyone is from Africa.

ALL turn and look at JORDAN.

JAMAL MAKAMBE YATES IS COMING TO DINNER

We follow the dog to ...

... a wealthy home in contemporary West Vancouver: living room, office, and a beautiful terrace. Summertime. The front door opens.

MOM: (*offstage*) Alice! Darling! Are you here?

MOM enters wearing a dashiki and colourful tights.

ALICE enters and embraces MOM.

ALICE: Oh Mother! (*beat*) Look at your face ... what's the matter?

MOM: My darling, what are you doing home? Susanna gave me the message that you'd stopped by our Tesla dealership. I just couldn't believe it! You weren't supposed to arrive until this evening. Did something happen?

ALICE: Yes, Mother. Something did happen.

MOM: (*grabbing at her face in desperation*) Oh what, Alice? What? Tell me!

ALICE: Sit down, if you don't mind. I'm dizzy. I'm absolutely dizzy with excitement.

MOM: Dizzy? Excitement? Have you been mixing Valium with alcohol again? You really shouldn't, darling. I know the numbness is everything, but you really can't get used to taking it that way.

ALICE: It's not the Valium.

MOM: The Lunesta?

ALICE: No, Mother –

MOM: (*interrupting*) You're staying for dinner, aren't you?

ALICE: I'm not staying for dinner, Mother. There just simply isn't enough time for any of that!

MOM: There would be if you saw the edible flowers I've got prepared, darling. They look like Brussels sprouts, but they're actually a rare species of begonia. They're utterly fabulous, Alice!

ALICE: (*upset*) Oh, Mother! Must you go on about begonias again?

MOM: I'm sorry, I'm sorry. They're just so versatile! (*beat*) What's happening? Do you need a Valium?

MOM gestures towards a candy dish on the coffee table that's full of anti-anxiety medication.

ALICE: I shouldn't.

MOM: What's two Valiums, darling? What's two or three? It's the world, isn't it? On fire and all of that ...

MOM throws a couple of pills in her mouth and swallows them. No water needed.

ALICE: Don't you see? Can't you *see* me? I'm not anxious anymore. I'm not tired or helpless or suddenly cruel to children. I'm happy. MOTHER, I'M SO HAPPY.

MOM stands up, her eyes glistening with tears.

MOM: Oh Alice. I did notice. I did. But I don't know why.

ALICE: There's three reasons why: Jamal Makambe Yates. (*bursting*) He's the most wonderful man I've ever met!

MOM: Oh, Alice. He sounds so utterly, authentically urban with a splash of unexpected wealth and privilege tacked on at the end. I'm thrilled! I just want to twist the beads of my hand-sewn dashiki, but it's so delicately woven I mustn't – I mustn't!

ALICE: But there's one thing. He has this awful idea that you'll hate him.

MOM: You told him, didn't you? About our principles? Our relish in cultures? Our foundations, our scholarships, our mint collection of Spike Lee films? Why would I hate him?

ALICE: He thinks you'll hate him because he's –

JAMAL enters the living room. MOM is shocked.

ALL: Caucasian.

JAMAL: (*approaching carefully*) Hello, Mrs. Newsbury ...

JAMAL reaches out to take MOM's hand. She accepts, gingerly.

MOM: Hello ...

ALICE: (*softly*) I had Tipsy make us up some sandwiches and coffee. We can all move to the terrace and have lunch. What do you say?

MOM: Yes, yes, all right ...

ALICE: We have to be quick about it.

MOM: Why?

JAMAL: I'm leaving tonight, you see, Mrs. Newsbury. Back to Washington for a conference on Tolkien.

ALICE: But ...

JAMAL: But before then ... we're –

ALICE: (*bursting*) We're getting married!

MOM: Oh!

ALICE: At city hall!

MOM: Oh! Oh!

JAMAL: If you approve, of course.

ALICE: Of course she approves. She's progressive! Aren't you, Mother?

MOM: Well yes, I ... does your father know?

ALICE: No, where is he?

We hear the sound of a car driving by.

JAMAL: I think I hear a car coming.

MOM: Oh no, love. You wouldn't *hear* a Tesla.

MOM and ALICE share a chuckle.

JAMAL: Right.

ALICE: Electric.

JAMAL: Yes.

MOM: You plug them in. No gas.

The front door opens.

ALICE: That must be Daddy now! Go on the terrace, Jamal!

JAMAL: Alice, maybe we should ease him into things. Please?

ALICE: Don't be ridiculous. Go, go, go, go.

> *ALICE shoves JAMAL out on the terrace as DAD comes into the living room wearing a Howard University hoodie, basketball shorts, knee-high socks, and sneakers.*

Alice! My dear! You're early!

ALICE: Daddy, there's someone I want you to meet. Let's go to the terrace.

DAD: All right! I don't mind meeting new people. In fact, our society depends on first impressions. I live for them. What will they be like, what will they say, will their hands be clammy, will they reach out for a shake?

> *MOM, DAD, and ALICE move to the terrace.*

DAD: And there's a huge misconception about the handshake, I'll have you know. I hired a man with a pitiful handshake. It was like holding on to a Slinky that had been put under some kind of Vaseline wash: LIMP. (*beat*) He was the best goddamn worker I ever had ...

MOM: Dear, this is Jamal Makambe Yates.

DAD: Oh hello, Jamal.

JAMAL: Hello, sir.

DAD: Curious collection of names you have there.

JAMAL: Yes, my parents were endlessly curious about other religions and cultures – Islam, Africa, Zimbabwe especially.

ALICE: Obviously.

JAMAL: So when I was old enough to change my middle name, I did. I lost Frederick and went with Makambe after my favourite racehorse. I'm afraid I didn't have much of a choice with the great big thud of my English surname ...

DAD: It's a bit like macramé, your name. Isn't it, Mom?

MOM: (*with her mouth full of sandwich*) Yes.

DAD: We were going to rename Alice Beyoncé, but we thought it might be a little gauche given the popularity of the *I Am ... Sasha Fierce* album and all.

>   DAD *takes a moment to reflect.*

What a liberating celebration of Black womanhood!

MOM: Dear, take a seat.

DAD: Ta-ta-ta. No time. I'm about to play hoops with (*with exaggerated emphasis on the accurate pronunciation*) Kenji, Wei Long, and Dr. Arsh Prajdeep. And I'm playing in Howard University's name, so if you'll excuse me, Jamal ...

ALICE: (*to Mom*) But Mother. He can't go.

MOM: (*to Dad*) Love, why don't you call them and say you're going to be a touch late?

DAD: Late? Me? Are you drunk?

MOM: But ... it's Jamal. Jamal's here. With us. Now. And for you to play now ... maybe not?

ALICE: (*frothing at the mouth*) Tell him, Jamal! Tell him!

JAMAL: I ... okay ... so ... here it is ... I ... (*blurting it out*) I fell in love with your daughter. And as incredible as it might seem ... she fell in love with me.

DAD: You did *what*?

ALICE: That's right! It never occurred to me that I'd fall in love with a Caucasian, but I did! And nothing in the world is going to change that!

JAMAL: (*to Dad*) Unless you don't approve, and then I'll disappear.

ALICE: Don't be ridiculous, Jamal! Even if Daddy did have objections, I wouldn't let you go ... not even if he were the mayor of Lothlórien!

DAD: But ... we sent you to Howard University. How the hell did you even find this guy?

ALICE: He's a professor!

DAD: At Howard University? Is that decent?

MOM: We didn't see any Caucasians in the brochures. And I don't skim. I'm quite thorough when it comes to pamphlets.

JAMAL: I teach English literature.

DAD: At Howard University?

JAMAL: Yes.

DAD: But ... !

JAMAL: With a focus on Tolkien.

DAD: TOLKIEN????

MOM: I don't understand.

DAD: A focus on Tolkien ... a *focus*, you said?

MOM: I'm sure Tolkien kept slaves. I'm sure of it.

ALICE: Jamal's lectures on Elven are exquisite.

JAMAL: Pedin i phith in aníron, a nin ú-cheniog.[1]

MOM and DAD watch in horror.

ALICE: Gellon ned i cenin i chent gîn ned i hol.[2]

JAMAL: (*correcting her*) GLA-dhol.

ALICE: Goheno nin. Gi melin.[3]

JAMAL: Gi melin. (*beat*) Well, do you have any objections, sir?

DAD: To the fantasy genre? No. It's a great platform to exercise metaphors of inclusivity of races.

JAMAL: I meant ... to Alice and I.

ALICE: Daddy! Hurry! We're getting married!

DAD: What?!

ALICE: Why else would I be wearing this charming little hat?

MOM: You often wear small hats, Alice!

---

1 I can say what I wish, and you can't understand.
2 I love to see your eyes when you laugh.
3 Forgive me. I love you.

DAD: What the hell is the rush?

JAMAL: With your approval, of course.

ALICE: No, Jamal.

JAMAL: Yes.

ALICE: No.

JAMAL: Yes.

MOM: Yes.

ALICE: Mom!

MOM: No.

ALICE: No.

JAMAL: Yes.

ALICE: NO.

JAMAL: Yes.

DAD: NO!! NO. I won't give you my approval. I FORBID THIS!

Pause.

DAD: I need a moment. I'll be inside.

DAD walks away, dribbling a basketball as he goes. He's actually pretty good.

ALICE: (*whining*) Mama! Do something!

MOM: All right. Pass me three ... no! ... *seven* tuna sandwiches.

ALICE and JAMAL pile sandwiches into MOM's hands.
MOM follows DAD inside.

MOM: Honey, I know this is all very sudden.

DAD: (*softening*) Are those ... seven tuna sandwiches?

> *DAD eats one and looks out the window at*
> *ALICE and JAMAL.*

DAD: Look at them out there.

MOM: What are they playing?

DAD: (*in disgust*) Cribbage.

MOM: Oh shit, goddamn! We tried to raise our child with an intersectional understanding of the world. To know that racism is real. Alice took that message of equality and measuring people on the strength of their character as individuals to the bank. We did *not* add: don't go and fall in love with a white man.

DAD: We certainly did not.

MOM: She was always a happy human being as a being. She laughed out loud at the touring production of *The Lion King* when she was eight weeks old. I swear ... in between her goo-goos and ga-gas she said, "Nants ingonyama bagithi Baba!"

DAD: She has no idea what she's doing. Sure, love, sure! But things aren't the way they used to be. Think of the missed opportunities. The social considerations. No one gives a shit about white babies! Every time I turn on the television, there's some cereal commercial with an interracial family and it's just undeniable! Those corkscrew curls! I wanted some kind of *real* athlete in the family. We're all athletic hobbyists doing layups while others soar above our heads and dunk! (*beat*) What nationality is he, even?

MOM: I think she said German.

DAD: Oh, the humanity! What will Alice and professor Schnitzel Baggins over there possibly have to talk about?

MOM: I approve.

DAD: You do?

MOM: Sort of, yes! Yes! No. Oh shit, goddamn! Why not? Actually ... maybe not. Oh fuck, who cares? Yes! No! Yes! No! /Yes! No!

JAMAL and ALICE enter.

JAMAL: /Mr. Newsbury, Mrs. Newsbury. Sorry to interrupt. I hope you won't find me forward, but I wanted to share something with all of you. Would you mind?

JAMAL, ALICE, MOM, and DAD go into the living room.

JAMAL: I just got a notification on my phone that my results came in from Ancestry.com. I've been doing some digging into my past, lots to unpack, but I'm hopeful.

ALICE: Read it! Read it!

JAMAL pulls up the results on his phone.

JAMAL: 47 percent Eastern European.

DAD: Well, yeah.

MOM: To be expected.

ALICE: Keep going, love.

JAMAL: (*tearing up*) 3 percent ... *Other Regions.*

ALICE, MOM, and DAD howl with excitement.

ALICE: /AHHHHHHHH!

MOM: /YES! YES! YES!

DAD: Three? That's practically its own pie!

JAMAL: There's more.

MOM: But how?

ALICE: Well, so far we're at 50 percent of a person, Mom.

JAMAL looks gutted.

ALICE: Darling?

JAMAL: 20 percent ... Great Britain ...

DAD throws a lamp against the window.

DAD: NO! NO! NO! (*beat*) NO!

MOM crumples to the floor.

MOM: The original colonizers ...

JAMAL drops his phone.

ALICE: Jamal ...

JAMAL: No. Stop. They're right. I'm not interesting. I don't mean to buy loose-fitting pants. These are slim-cut! My pancake-flat ass could fit inside a wallet. (*showing them*) Look at it! LOOK AT IT!!!

DAD: Dear God ... you could play snooker off that rump ...

MOM: That's all right. We enjoy bangers and mash on occasion ...

JAMAL: No, it's not all right. I'll go. Novaer.[4]

JAMAL gets up to leave. ALICE picks up his phone, determined.

ALICE: No! Look! Jamal! There's another slice ...

MOM: What does it say, Alice?

ALICE: Oh my God ... oh my God ... 0.5 percent ... AFRICAN AMERICAN!

ALL erupt in a cheer, lifting JAMAL up like he's just won a championship.

MOM: (*screaming, jumping, screaming*) YES! YES! YES!

DAD: I sensed it, you know. I felt altogether tribal around him. I could hear his heart, thrumming along like a djembe. My own was trying to keep rhythm with his, but it couldn't keep pace.

MOM: You know, Jamal, your nose, it always seemed so delectably flat – like a misshapen strawberry.

JAMAL: You know what this means, Big Daddy, don't you? Alumni basketball!

MOM: Breakdancing! How's your toprock?

DAD: Jamal "Crazy Legs" Macambe Yates!

JAMAL turns away suddenly, looking very sad.

ALICE: Jamal? Are you all right?

---

4 Farewell.

JAMAL: You know. I'm sorry, everyone. I'm just reflecting on Denzel Washington and how long it took for him to win an Oscar for us.

MOM: Son, don't apologize for being moved by our people overcoming adversity.

DAD: We're all with it, ya dig?

ALICE: We all dig!

MOM: Why don't we all skip city hall and jump the broom?

ALL: YES! Of course!

> ALL start dancing wildly to drums as the lights snap to black.

WHAT KIND OF DOG IS THAT?
PART 4

Mike and Marissa's condo. GERALD watches a video on his phone.

GERALD: (*to Mike*) Bruh, look at this.

GERALD shows MIKE his phone. They erupt in laughter.

MIKE: Ooops!

AISHA: Ooooh, let me see that.

GERALD tilts the phone so that AISHA can see. MARISSA and JORDAN crane their heads to look, not getting an invitation.

AISHA: If fuck-around-and-find-out was a person.

MIKE: Seek and you shall FIND!

GERALD: Oh, homeboy found more than what he was looking for. He found Jesus. Bro bro smacked the devil out of him.

AISHA: In the name of JESUS, I liberate that evil spirit out of your body!

MIKE: Praise BE!

GERALD: Should have ordered that shut up with a side of mind your own business.

MIKE: Ordered that two piece instead and got some lumps for free!

AISHA: Got the whole combo: SUPER-SIZED!

*MIKE, GERALD, and AISHA laugh hysterically. MARISSA
and JORDAN laugh, too, because they feel left out and don't
really understand.*

MARISSA: What's so funny?

MIKE: Don't worry about it.

MARISSA: What do you mean?

MIKE: It's just not for you.

MARISSA: (*to Jordan*) It's not for us, Jordan.

GERALD: In a way, I'm jealous.

AISHA: Jealous of what?

GERALD: Of how free they are.

JORDAN: Of how free who are?

MIKE, GERALD, and AISHA ignore JORDAN and keep going.

GERALD: I'm serious. There's a level of confidence required to run
your mouth any type of way to anyone. I wish I could …

MIKE: I don't take shit off of anyone. Ever.

GERALD: Taking shit off of people is what I do for a living.

AISHA: I deflect any negativity that comes my way with
strategic side-eye.

GERALD: I see those side-eyes. It kills me to see my woman
disrespected and I can't do anything about it.

MIKE: When Marissa feels disrespected, my biggest concern is holding her back so she doesn't land herself in jail.

MARISSA: Okay, what are you saying about me now?

MIKE: That you're insane. One time, you called that Dollarama security guard a "fascist fuckhead" for following me around.

MARISSA: He was both of those things. And he was following you around.

MIKE: Which I guess is your point, G.

AISHA: Yup. They're free, like, fully free.

GERALD: Even as a cop, with a good salary and a nice car, in a good neighbourhood –

AISHA: And a fine-ass, sophisticated, entrepreneurial woman by your side.

GERALD: No doubt, baby, but even with all of that, I'm always aware that I'm one mistake away from losing everything.

JORDAN: Amen, brother.

AISHA: Hey. Wonder Bread. You're still in time out. Sit there and think about how much you miss the rains down in Africa, Toto ...

JORDAN: See, one mistake!

MARISSA: Can we let it go? He didn't mean it like that.

JORDAN: I wasn't implying ...

MIKE: (*interrupting*) That we were all Black?

JORDAN: No, that /race is a social construct.

AISHA: /That what? Race doesn't exist?

MARISSA: Stop interrupting him! Jordan – go ahead.

JORDAN: Well no, but biologically it doesn't.

MARISSA: Oh Jesus ...

GERALD, MIKE, and AISHA let out exasperated sighs.

JORDAN: WHAT?

AISHA: We were explaining that humankind originated in Africa. Not that everyone is Black, you out-of-context quoting motherfucker.

JORDAN: Okay, well, you know what, Aisha? Technically, race is a social construct. Right, Marissa?

MARISSA: Nope, don't bring me into this.

AISHA: Yeah, uh-huh, and I suppose white privilege is also a social construct?

JORDAN: Yeah, actually. I grew up in a literal trailer park. We were like the Black people of the white people in our neighbourhood.

AISHA: What the fuck?

MIKE: Did you smoke before coming here? Are you high right now?

JORDAN: No, asshole, I'm five years sober and you know that – fuck you.

GERALD: /Let's chill out.

AISHA: /WHOA!

MARISSA: /Guys!

AISHA: The condo king is talking about how privilege is made up. The cluelessness is real!

JORDAN: If you keep blaming society for holding you back, you'll keep being right.

AISHA: What in the Tony Robbins are you on about?

JORDAN: It's TRUE. I'm not saying racism isn't real, it IS, but it's not the reason you're paying rent in New West, and I've got tenants paying my mortgage in West Van.

MARISSA: /Jesus. Nobody cares!

MIKE: /Shut up, Jordan.

GERALD: (*to Aisha*) Don't bite, Aisha.

AISHA: No, please, tell us more about what's racist and what's not, trailer park Jo-jo from down in the Bayou.

JORDAN: Yeah, no, make fun of the guy who grew up poor. I'm sure that's what you did at your fancy college!

AISHA: /I went to SFU, you fucking idiot!

MIKE: /You're not fucking poor anymore!

AISHA: I need another drink.

MARISSA: No, you definitely don't, Aisha.

AISHA: The fuck I don't!

MARISSA: It's just ... you got drunk at our place last time and our neighbours complained.

MIKE: She's right. You also puked on our coffee table and obliterated our wine glasses.

JORDAN: I was also a witness to this.

AISHA: Oh, I guess I'm just the loud-ass Black woman /that needs to be checked, huh?

MARISSA: /That's not what we meant!

MIKE: /We didn't say that.

AISHA: /Coming in here, breaking all those fancy Ikea wine glasses!

MARISSA: (*defensively*) Uh, nice try. They were from the Bay.

AISHA: Fuck your wine glass!

    AISHA breaks a wine glass.

GERALD: Easy, baby.

MIKE: So we're intentionally breaking glasses now?

    GERALD picks up the broken glass with MARISSA.

AISHA: That's right. I'm causing mischief stone-cold sober.

MARISSA: (*to Aisha*) I would ask you to clean up the glass, but I don't want to be accused of oppressing you.

AISHA: /Oh, it's like that?

MARISSA: /You threw a fucking wine glass!

MIKE: (*to Gerald*) Yo, control your girl.

GERALD: /Excuse me?

AISHA: /Bitch, control your mouth!

MARISSA: That's not insulting at all, Mike.

MIKE: Huh? I'm sorry, what are you mad at now?

MARISSA: Oh, this is the part where you accuse me of being moody and emotional?

MIKE: You are emotional. All the time.

MARISSA: Well then leave! I don't own you! Go anytime!

MIKE: Oh, that was right on the tip of your tongue, wasn't it?

JORDAN: Come on, Mike. That's ridiculous. This is ridiculous!

MARISSA: Seriously, Mike, what do you want? An apology?

MIKE: Yeah. I do.

MARISSA: FOR WHAT?

MIKE: White supremacy!

AISHA: That sounds good, actually.

MARISSA: Yeah, you know what? It's coming in the mail alongside your apology for the patriarchy and your apology to my glass cabinet! Which is now uneven!

GERALD: ENOUGH. Stop. STOP talking. What the fuck is happening? Is this what hanging out consists of these days? Lectures and fucking keywords? Everyone stop and just breathe.

Pause.

MIKE: Some of us can't breathe.

AISHA: Mike, don't …

MIKE: What? The pig is entering the conversation now?

    ALL react.

GERALD: (*under his breath*) This motherfucker …

JORDAN: White dudes. Karen. The pig.

MARISSA: He's got shitty, dismissive labels for everybody.

MIKE: (*resolutely*) That's right.

JORDAN: So this is it. This is the way it is? Mike and Aisha get to
    say and do whatever they want – they get to be peak them – and
    the rest of us can't even blink without getting blasted.

AISHA: For another three hundred years. Yes.

JORDAN: What the fuck is your problem?

AISHA: My problem is I have a little eager white boy nipping at my
    heels every second I change directions – "Did I do that right?
    Did I say that right? Look, look, I read one Black article in a
    decade! Let me quote it for you!"

JORDAN: I read everything you send in our group chat! You don't
    take me seriously. All you do is humiliate me! For trying!

AISHA: Try away from me. Spare me the disappointment
    that is *you.*

JORDAN: No problem, *girlfriend.*

AISHA: Oh, I'm about to clear that glass /cabinet on your head …

JORDAN: /I'm sorry, I'm sorry. I thought it would come out
    much softer.

MARISSA: Okay, everybody just stop before this gets way out of hand.

MIKE: Don't worry. Things get out of hand, Officer Gerald here will just start shooting the Black people.

AISHA: Fuck off, Mike.

GERALD: (*to Mike*) Man, I wasn't raised to speak ill of people, especially when I'm standing in their home. But you're a self-centred asshole, Mike.

JORDAN: Guys, come on.

GERALD: No, he needs to hear it.

MIKE: Please. Tell me what I need to hear, pig.

MARISSA: Mike, STOP saying that.

GERALD: You're a textbook narcissist.

AISHA: (*to Gerald*) Baby ...

MIKE: (*scoffing*) I'm a narcissist.

GERALD: All you do is talk. Talk, talk, talk. We all have to listen to your stories about your day – how you feel about everything. You don't have the interesting take all the time!

MIKE: But your basic police bros have profound insights of the human condition.

GERALD: Fucking Christ. You just have to make sure that everybody knows you're an educated Black man.

AISHA: Mhmmm ...

GERALD: White people this. White people that. You married a
   white woman.

MIKE: So?

GERALD: So what does that say about you? You either hate
   yourself or you hate Marissa and got married to punish her.
   Either way, shut the fuck up about it for five seconds.

MARISSA: How about we all shut the fuck up about me and
   my marriage?

AISHA: You married a Black man, sweetie.

MARISSA: /Sweetie?

JORDAN: /What are you implying?

AISHA: Here comes Jo-Jo! Always right there to defend Marissa.

JORDAN: I need a pit bull to defend Marissa from you.

MARISSA: Leave it, Jordan.

MIKE: (*to Gerald*) Look, I don't know who you think you're
   talking to –

GERALD: I'm talking to *you*.

MIKE: Well, I'm not the one.

GERALD: You act like you're the only one that matters.

MIKE: You act like nothing matters to you.

GERALD: Lots of things matter. When you deal with REAL
   problems, you don't have to reach for imaginary ones.

MIKE: So, systemic racism is imaginary? Gotcha.

GERALD: No. It's VERY real. I just don't have time for privileged-ass people with a victim mentality.

MIKE: I'm nobody's victim.

GERALD: Well, you sure act like one. We live in Vancouver, one of the most beautiful cities in the world. You have a healthy brain and body, a wife that loves you for some reason, a good job.

MIKE: I'm not talking to a Black fucking conservative/

AISHA: /He's not conservative!

MIKE: – that regurgitates FOX NEWS talking points.

GERALD: I would rather be called a Black conservative than be associated with this hotep bullshit.

JORDAN: /What? What's a hotep?

MARISSA: /We have neighbours!

MIKE: /Good. Keep tap dancing for your po-po overlords.

MARISSA: Mike!

GERALD: And you keep tapping on your little keyboard, posting about cops as if you know what goes on. You think I don't see the shit you post?

MIKE: Good! You should read ALL my shit. Learn something. Start with the quotes from parents talking about their kids being shot by cops.

GERALD: You know what, man? You think that shit doesn't disturb me?

MIKE: Apparently not.

GERALD: You think I don't feel like there's a spotlight on my fucking face when they talk about BLM in the lunchroom? I'm one of the only Black officers in the entire city.

MIKE: Ever ask yourself WHY that is?

GERALD: I know why! Assholes like you who think every shitty cop on CNN represents every cop, even in Canada.

MIKE: It DOES! You are part of a racist SYSTEM! You should speak up!

GERALD: I DO! I also have to balance being the mouthpiece for all Black people with keeping my fucking job!

MIKE: /Your job, your job – your job is not an excuse.

GERALD: /Without being labelled soft. With maintaining my very thin status as part of the brotherhood.

MIKE: Those are your brothers?

GERALD: Being on time. Being good at my job. Being respectful.

MIKE: Christ ... you really believe this.

GERALD: Being appreciative. This is how I survive, you self-righteous fuck!

MIKE: I'm loyal to my community, not my job!

AISHA: /So am I! So is he!

GERALD: /OUR Community! I'm also a Black man?

MIKE: Glad you still realize it.

GERALD: I worked my ass off to get where I – am.

MIKE: The ol' bootstraps argument – classic.

GERALD: And I didn't have a mom and dad – to get me through.

MIKE: Don't talk about my mom!

GERALD: Nigga, fuck your mom!

AISHA: /Gerald!

MARISSA: /Guys!

JORDAN: /Hey!

GERALD: /and FUCK YOU!

MIKE: FUCK YOU, YOU FUCKING COON!

> *Pause.*

MARISSA: What the hell, Mike?

> *GERALD grabs his coat. AISHA looks at MIKE before leaving.*

THE BLACK AGENDA

We follow the dog to ...

... Black headquarters in the future. A black hole in space.

Ship's log is played as a voiceover as COMRADE BLACK and COMRADE BLACKITY BLACK take what appear to be COVID tests. They swab their noses and put the tests in a suction tube labelled "Blackness Test." They are dressed like Afro-Futurists (think Black Panther meets Star Trek: The Next Generation). *KAREN is imprisoned (perhaps in a cage-like construction made out of tribalesque spears).*

VOICEOVER: (*COMRADE BLACK's voice*) Comrade's log, woke date two, twenty-eight, forty-five. We have completed the third and final stage of the Great Cancellation. We, the voyagers aboard the Black Starline, have successfully cleansed the world of all overt and covert racists. Gone are the klansmen and neo-nazis. Missing are the crooked cops, judges, bank managers, and shitty landlords. Our ship's computer, Garvey, the collective consciousness of what was once Black Twitter's algorithm, has brought us to an undisclosed location in space where we can take our final Blackness test and await the results. Once this step is complete, we can finally rest, knowing that those who fucked around found out, and those who found out will no longer be the fuck around here as they found the fuck out.

COMRADE BLACK: Where are we on the map, Comrade Blackity Black?

COMRADE BLACKITY BLACK: Hard to tell, Comrade Black. Black holes are a little more fucked up than your average hole. For instance, yesterday we believed that by using the hole's own gravitational energy, we could maneuver ourselves against it like a slingshot – creating a bit of a heave-ho situation.

COMRADE BLACK: Did we, Comrade Blackity Black?

COMRADE BLACKITY BLACK: Negative, Comrade Black. It seems we have plunged further down into what we believe is the nexus of the black hole. Now it appears that we're placed directly in the centre of it.

COMRADE BLACK: Demonstrate.

COMRADE BLACKITY BLACK moves to the right side of the ship, demonstrating his next point.

COMRADE BLACKITY BLACK: If I look out the window at the far end of the right side of the ship, I see blackness.

COMRADE BLACK: Excellent.

COMRADE BLACKITY BLACK moves to the left side of the ship, demonstrating his point.

COMRADE BLACKITY BLACK: Similarly, if I look out the window at the far end of the left side of the ship, I see the same amount of blackness.

COMRADE BLACK: So it's official. We're in the blackest place in the universe.

COMRADE BLACKITY BLACK: Sho'nuff, Comrade Black.

COMRADE BLACK: Respect, Comrade Blackity Black! We've done it. The Great Cancellation is a success. It's taken years, but here we are. Once we get the results back from our Blackness test, we can recharge over a game of dominoes and reruns of *The Jeffersons.*

COMRADE BLACKITY BLACK and COMRADE BLACK: Sho'nuff!

KAREN: (*from her cage*) Madame Black?

COMRADE BLACK: NOT NOW, Karen.

KAREN: Sorry, I've just thought of another thing I have to apologize for. When I was five years old, my mother gave me the option of a Black doll or a white doll and instead of choosing the Black doll, I chose the white doll.

COMRADE BLACK: That's fairly standard white fuckery, Karen.

KAREN: (*welling up*) Yes, but then I got the Black doll for my birthday and when I engaged in imaginative play, the Black doll was relegated to roles such as sassy best friend, social worker, and wig maker and she only made it to second base with California Ken even though I knew she wanted to go the whole way.

COMRADE BLACK: Save your tears, Karen. We'll need them.

KAREN: Sho'nuff.

A very "Black" alarm (possibly reggae style) rings out.

COMRADE BLACKITY BLACK: Is that?/

COMRADE BLACK: /The racism alarm?!

COMRADE BLACKITY BLACK: But ... it can't be? We've cancelled all of the racists!

GARVEY: Bitch. That alarm won't answer itself. Step to it.

COMRADE BLACKITY BLACK: Apologies, Garvey.

COMRADE BLACK: We're on it. It won't happen again.

> *COMRADE BLACKITY BLACK stands in front of a giant motherboard. The tech looks like a sophisticated version of the game* Frogger.

GARVEY: Incoming colonizer.

GARVEY displays a file on a man named Roger.

COMRADE BLACKITY BLACK: Garvey is sending us a white named Roger. In his fifties. Current CEO of a renewable-energy plant.

We see a still image of Roger bent over a Red Lobster bucket of crab legs. He's wearing a bib and his face has a substantial amount of butter sauce on it. His eyes are closed. He's enjoying his meal very much.

COMRADE BLACK: Those crab legs ain't sustainable, I'll tell you that much.

COMRADE BLACKITY BLACK: How did we miss him?

GARVEY: Last name Jones. Connected to South Carolina slavers circa 1838. Uploading his list of crimes to your comms systems now.

COMRADE BLACK: Let's beam him up.

COMRADE BLACKITY BLACK: How much you wanna bet he comes up here mid-golf swing, looking like Arnold Palmer?

We hear a loud laser sound and see a beam of light. ROGER is on the ship in full golf gear, mid-swing.

ROGER: FORE!

It takes ROGER a second before he realizes he's not on the golf course anymore.

ROGER: Oh God. It's happening.

COMRADE BLACK: Roger, our systems have run a check on your surname and we've detected a flair for colonialism.

ROGER: I know! I know! I've very recently discovered my family's horrible history and I've dedicated the past eight to twelve months to atoning for those sins!

COMRADE BLACKITY BLACK: Yes, we're aware. The reason you've been brought here is actually to discuss the summer internships you ran as part of your company's "diversity" initiative.

ROGER: Oh! Yes! Corners to Coding? You've heard of my efforts to bring tech to inner-city youth!

COMRADE BLACK: Since your company moved into the Gastown area, rents have quadrupled. Inner-city youth don't need internships. They need radical change.

KAREN: BURN HIM!

ROGER: But surely I'm not to be blamed for the gentrification of Vancouver. That's a very layered, complex issue.

COMRADE BLACKITY BLACK: (*warningly*) You're rationalizing, Roger ...

ROGER: (*sincerely*) Okay. All right. I will do whatever it takes to make this right and prove that I am a true and loyal ally. What do I have to do? Just tell me.

COMRADE BLACK: Effective immediately, you will forfeit your land and home and step down as CEO/of your company.

ROGER: What the fuck? But ... it's my company. Jones *and* sons. This is our family legacy, built from scratch. My grandparents fled Germany with nothing, and –

KAREN: FASCIST!

ROGER: No. We *fled* the fascists! We were fleeing.

KAREN: FUCKING PIG!

COMRADE BLACK: Hand over the reins to one of the inner-city youth from your summer internship.

ROGER: (*beat*) Okay ... but ... they're all still very much learning ... (*beat*) Can I at least keep my stock options?

KAREN: ROAST HIM ALIVE! EAT THE RICH!

ROGER: Okay! Fine! I'LL GIVE IT ALL UP!

GARVEY: Ass-whooping complete.

ROGER is beamed back down.

COMRADE BLACKITY BLACK: Our next reparations candidate is Thomas Thompson.

COMRADE BLACK: Okay, let's see this profile. (*beat*) Wait, this must be some sort of glitch.

GARVEY: I'm never wrong, bitch-ass.

COMRADE BLACKITY BLACK: Right, but it says here he's a Black man, a Morehouse graduate, a five-star general, and winner of the Nobel Peace Prize?

COMRADE BLACK: Well, that's just confusing –

COMRADE BLACKITY BLACK: An active member of the Big Brothers Big Sisters of America program, regular volunteer at his local soup kitchen, and finally, it says, "Loved his momma more than life itself." I don't get it ...?

COMRADE BLACK: I guess ... beam him up and we'll find out.

COMRADE BLACKITY BLACK does. TOM appears.

TOM: Greetings, friends. A pleasure to make your acquaintance.

COMRADE BLACKITY BLACK: (*beat*) Sup ...

TOM: I'm doing well, thanks. Tell me, why is it that I find myself aboard your famed vessel this evening?

COMRADE BLACK: You tell us.

TOM: All right. What would you like to know?

COMRADE BLACKITY BLACK: Um ... what were you up to this evening?

TOM: Well, after my regular evening shift at the soup kitchen, I went to tutor local youth at my old public high school. Then I went home to get ready to go out for supper with my African Queen, but not before placing fresh lilies on Mama's tombstone.

KAREN: How did she die? Because my aunt died once and I'm wondering if it was the same way.

COMRADE BLACKITY BLACK: Sorry that we disturbed you, sir. Have a wonderful evening.

COMRADE BLACK: WAIT ... where were you and your wife going to ... *supper*?

TOM: Why, a gorgeous banquet hall catered by a local Ethiopian restaurant for the annual Black Conservative Party meet up!

COMRADE BLACK: /There it is!

COMRADE BLACKITY BLACK: /There it is!

KAREN: STAB HIM!!!

COMRADE BLACKITY BLACK: Easy, Karen./

TOM: /What did I do wrong?

COMRADE BLACK: (*spitting*) You're a conservative!

TOM: But traditional conservative values made me the man
   I am today.

KAREN: (*hissing*) Verbum Domini Manet in Aeternum!

COMRADE BLACKITY BLACK: RENOUNCE CONSERVATISM!

COMRADE BLACK: BUT CONTINUE DOING THE POSITIVE
   THINGS THAT YOU DO IN SPITE OF IT!

TOM: But what's the dif –

KAREN: Identify as a Liberal DEMOCRAT, DINK!

TOM: Okay! Okay! I'll identify as a Liberal Democrat but change
   nothing about my behaviour, belief system, or daily routine?

COMRADE BLACK: Good! Beam him down.

   TOM is beamed down.

COMRADE BLACKITY BLACK: Our next reparations candid –

GARVEY: WARNING. WARNING. Fuel levels are critical.
   Extensive white tears are needed immediately.

   COMRADE BLACK looks at KAREN.

COMRADE BLACK: Now, Karen! It's time.

   KAREN nods and stands up.

KAREN: Play the 911 call I placed in 2012.

   COMRADE BLACKITY BLACK types into the motherboard.

GARVEY: There are twenty-six 911 calls registered under your name in that year.

KAREN: (*like Clint Eastwood*) Dealer's choice.

> *COMRADE BLACKITY BLACK chooses one and plays it over the ship's sound system. The ship begins struggling or shaking.*

VOICEOVER: 911, what's your emergency?

> *KAREN stands, eyes closed, listening to her own 911 call. She's powering up.*

VOICEOVER (*Karen's voice*): Yes, hello?

VOICEOVER: Hi, can you hear me?

VOICEOVER (*Karen's voice*): Yes, hello? I've been attacked!

> *Pieces of the ship's ceiling are falling now. COMRADE BLACK and COMRADE BLACKITY BLACK duck for cover. KAREN holds her ground, listening, harnessing.*

VOICEOVER: You've been attacked?

VOICEOVER (*Karen's voice*): Yes! This man and his pit bull attacked my chihuahua!

VOICEOVER (*male voice*): That's not a pit bull ...

VOICEOVER (*Karen's voice*): OW! OW!

VOICEOVER: Ma'am? Ma'am, are you okay?

VOICEOVER (*Karen's voice*): AH! HELP! HE JUST BIT ME!

VOICEOVER (*male voice*): No, he didn't?

VOICEOVER (*Karen's voice*): Yes, he did! Ah! He has a gun! Help!

VOICEOVER (*male voice*): What are you talking about? I don't have a gun. She's lying!

> *The ship shakes and begins to tilt. COMRADE BLACK and COMRADE BLACKITY BLACK slide towards the engine room.*

COMRADE BLACK: KAREN! NOW!

VOICEOVER: Ma'am? Are you there?

> *It's KAREN who is shaking now. An anime-style power-up transformation occurs. KAREN extends her arms and opens her mouth wide – a beam of white light comes out of every orifice as she cries out He-Man style (think "I have the power").*

KAREN: I AM SO – SOOOOOORRRRY!!!!

> *The lights on the ship start flashing wildly. A song like "A Thousand Miles" by Vanessa Carlton plays as well as other white singers' covers of Black artists' songs. It's sound and visual overload.*

> *COMRADE BLACKITY BLACK and COMRADE BLACK cover their eyes.*

> *Blackout.*

> *After a moment, a chirpy, happy sound plays.*

> *Lights power back up. KAREN is on the floor in the fetal position, completely drained.*

GARVEY: White-tear levels are back to full capacity. Fuel cells restored.

COMRADE BLACK rushes to KAREN and bends down.

COMRADE BLACK: You did good, Karen.

KAREN turns to face COMRADE BLACK.

KAREN: (*faintly*) ... Pinot Gris ...

COMRADE BLACK: Comrade Blackity Black! The Pinot Grigio!

KAREN: ... Gris ... not Grigio ...

COMRADE BLACKITY BLACK gets KAREN a glass of Pinot Gris.

KAREN: ... Mmmm ... Kim Crawford. Thank you.

The Black alarm goes off again.

GARVEY: Colonizers located aboard vessel.

COMRADE BLACK: /What?

COMRADE BLACKITY BLACK: /But how?

GARVEY: Uploading profiles now.

We hear the sounds of information being uploaded to the motherboard. Photos of Comrade Black and Comrade Blackity Black appear on the screen.

COMRADE BLACKITY BLACK: Wait ... this can't be right?

COMRADE BLACK: We failed the Black test?

GARVEY: Affirmative, you Oreo motherfuckers.

COMRADE BLACK: But ... we're very Black!

COMRADE BLACKITY BLACK: Like, literally blackity Black.

COMRADE BLACK: Like, James Baldwin meets Angela Davis Black.

KAREN: (*pouring more wine*) Like a hockey puck!

COMRADE BLACK and COMRADE BLACKITY BLACK: NO, KAREN!

> *COMRADE BLACKITY BLACK and COMRADE BLACK look at each other.*

COMRADE BLACKITY BLACK: It was her! I saw her clap her hands to the *Friends* theme song!

> *KAREN gasps.*

COMRADE BLACK: You're the one who has the box set! I was only borrowing it! (*beat*) OKAY THAT SONG IS KIND OF A BOP!

> *They all clap the* Friends *theme song.*

COMRADE BLACK: Yeah, well, when I offered him jerk chicken this afternoon, he said what he liked most about it was that it wasn't "too spicy."

> *KAREN tisk tisks.*

COMRADE BLACKITY BLACK: Because it wasn't! There was no flavour!

COMRADE BLACK: Take that back! Plenty of pimento in that sauce!

COMRADE BLACKITY BLACK: She dropped her phone the other day and I heard her say, "Whoopsie doodle."

> *KAREN gasps.*

COMRADE BLACK: And you caught it and said, "This isn't my first rodeo."

KAREN double gasps.

GARVEY: Whose mans is this? Beaming down in three ...

COMRADE BLACK: No! We can't go back there. It's a wasteland!

GARVEY: Two ...

COMRADE BLACKITY BLACK: Please! Let us take the test again!

KAREN: See ya later, alligators!

COMRADE BLACKITY BLACK and **COMRADE BLACK**
In a while, crocodile! (*beat*) SHITWHATTHEFUCK.

GARVEY: One.

COMRADE BLACKITY BLACK and COMRADE BLACK are beamed down. The ship is floating through space alone in silence. Then ...

KAREN: So, it's just us now eh, Garvey? Can we have some music? It's so quiet ... ooooh maybe some Motown?

GARVEY: Activate self-destruct mode.

The ship blows up.

WHAT KIND OF DOG IS THAT?
PART 5

English Bay. Sunny. MIKE and MARISSA sit on the same bench on the seawall as in Part 1.

MARISSA: What happened last night?

Pause.

MIKE: I don't know.

MIKE and MARISSA sit some more.

MARISSA: Have you checked in with Gerald?

MIKE: No.

MIKE and MARISSA sit some more.

MARISSA: Maybe you should?

MIKE: Yeah? And what am I going to say?

Pause.

MARISSA: I don't know.

MIKE and MARISSA sit some more.

JEFFREY: (*offstage, dreamlike*) John!

MIKE and MARISSA perk up. Was that ...?

JEFFREY: (*offstage*) John! Come!

MIKE: That dog. (*beat*) That dog ...

MIKE and MARISSA look at each other.

MIKE and MARISSA: (*together*) That *fucking* dog!

MIKE and MARISSA get up and chase after the dog.
We watch them run for a while.

Gradually, MIKE and MARISSA are joined by KAREN,
COMRADE BLACK, JAMAL, MR. JIMMY, and DOLLEY.

ALL run after the dog. It's desperate. They run, run, run –
beyond breath – run, run, run ...

Together, ALL follow the dog into darkness.

The end

ACKNOWLEDGMENTS

Our deepest thanks to the Canada Council for the Arts, the Arts Club Theatre Company, Tarragon Theatre, and Imago Theatre for supporting *Redbone Coonhound* through its rolling world premiere, and to all the artists and collaborators who were invaluable to its development. To Ashlie Corcoran and Stephen Drover who commissioned this play and were the heartbeat through the pandemic and beyond; to Micheline Chevrier for reading it and saying yes, for always seeing us; to Mike Payette for including this piece in your inaugural Tarragon season; to Kwaku Okyere and Jessie Liang for your incredible insights, collaboration, and joy; to Cristina Cugliandro for your endless encouragement and for helping make this play a reality on the East Coast; to Rena Zimmerman for always being there; to our families and friends for being our guiding light; and to the voices in the world and in the room that inspire us.

Amy Lee Lavoie is an award-winning playwright and graduate of the National Theatre School of Canada's Playwriting Program. Her first play, *Rabbit Rabbit*, won several awards and has been produced across Canada and the US. Amy Lee is currently developing a number of projects with her husband and collaborator Omari Newton, including an adaptation of *Titus Andronicus*, an opera adaptation of Dante's *Inferno*, and a new play for Geordie Theatre's 2024/2025 season.

photo by Kristine Cofsky

Omari Newton is an award-winning actor, writer, director, and head of the acting department at the Vancouver Film School. As a writer, his original hip hop theatre piece *Sal Capone* has received critical acclaim and multiple productions, including a recent presentation at Canada's National Arts Centre.

photo by Zuckermann & Wong

ELVEN (SINDARIN) PRONUNCIATION GUIDE

by Nina Houle

Sindarin doesn't have any silent letters; pronounce everything on the page. Stress falls on the second syllable of a two-syllable word or on the first syllable of a three-syllable word (for example, the first line begins "Pe-DITH i PHITH in A-ni-ron").

Vowel sounds: *A* as in "father," *E* as in "ending," *I* as in "machine," *O* as in "no." *U* is a bit pursed, as in the French word "lune."

Ch is pronounced as in the Scottish word "loch."

G sounds are always hard, as in "gull."

R is trilled or rolled, like the *R* sound in Spanish.

TH is pronounced as in "breathe" (as opposed to as in "breath").

REDBONE
COONHOUND
TEACHER RESOURCE
GUIDE

WELCOME

This guide was created for teachers and students. It contains an overview of the play's story as well as informative resources and activities for teachers and students. The guide aims to provide background knowledge and critical perspectives on the play that will yield fruitful discussion and foster an understanding and appreciation of the theatre arts.

This study guide was created for the Arts Club Theatre by Ceanna Wood and Natalie Davidson and is reprinted here in an edited version with permission.

LEARNING OBJECTIVES

After viewing *Redbone Coonhound* and engaging with some of the discussion questions and resources provided in this guide, students should be able to:

- Identify the use of satire and parody as literary devices in the play;
- Begin to engage in conversations about race, considering their own identities and how they might relate to the play or be challenged by it;
- Begin to understand the complexity and intersections of race and gender in interpersonal relationships;
- Identify how real-world topics and conflicts can drive story;
- Be able to engage critically with the process of theatrical adaptation of historic events.

CONNECTIONS TO NEW BC CURRICULUM

DRAMA 12

- Evaluate the social, cultural, historical, environmental, and personal contexts of dramatic works;
- Demonstrate personal and social responsibility associated with creating, performing, and responding to dramatic works;
- Examine the impacts of dramatic works on culture and society.

LITERARY STUDIES 12

- Understand and appreciate how different forms, formats, structures, and features of texts reflect a variety of purposes, audiences, and messages (for example, literary devices, like satire);
- Think critically, creatively, and reflectively to analyze ideas within, between, and beyond texts;
- Recognize and analyze personal, social, cultural contexts, values, and perspectives in texts, including culture, gender, sexual orientation, and socio-economic status.

20TH CENTURY WORLD HISTORY 12

- Compare and contrast continuities and changes for different groups at particular times and places (continuity and change);
- Assess how underlying conditions and the actions of individuals or groups affect events, decisions, and developments, and analyze multiple consequences (cause and consequence);
- Explain different perspectives on past or present people, places, issues, and events by considering prevailing norms, values, world-views, and beliefs (perspective);
- Make reasoned ethical judgments about controversial actions in the past or present and assess whether we have a responsibility to respond (ethical judgment).

ABOUT THE PLAYWRIGHTS:

AMY LEE LAVOIE AND OMARI NEWTON

Amy Lee Lavoie is an award-winning playwright and graduate of the National Theatre School of Canada's Playwriting Program. Her first play, *Rabbit Rabbit,* won several awards and has been produced across Canada and the US. Amy Lee is currently developing an original play, *Women Do Not Go on Strike,* and co-writing projects with her husband and collaborator Omari Newton, including an adaptation of *Titus Andronicus,* an adaptation of Dante's *Inferno,* and a new play for Geordie Theatre's 2024/2025 season.

Omari Newton is an award-winning actor, writer, director, and head of the acting department at the Vancouver Film School. As a writer, his original hip hop theatre piece *Sal Capone* has received critical acclaim and multiple productions, including a recent presentation at Canada's National Arts Centre.

SYNOPSIS:
REDBONE COONHOUND

Out for a walk in their neighbourhood in Vancouver's West End, Mike and Marissa – an interracial married couple – meet a dog with an unfortunate breed name: Redbone Coonhound. For context, the term "redbone" originated in Louisiana as a Cajun word for a lighter-skinned mixed-race person, but it is a disparaging description that feeds into colourism. The word "coon" is extremely offensive and comes from minstrel show characters like Zip Coon who were performed by white people in blackface that perpetuated contemptuous and derogatory stereotypes of Black people. Within the Black community today, the word is used to insult a Black person who allegedly acts in ways meant to gain favour from white people. As a Black man, Mike is understandably incensed by this name that contains these two racial slurs. Suddenly, the coonhound chases Mike into Stanley Park, and he transforms into his great-great-grandfather, who's trying to escape the American South and get to Canada via the Underground Railroad in 1840. This is the first of a series of "play provocations" within the play itself that travel through time and space. These provocations are satirical meditations on the ideas presented by the main storyline and are driven by either Marissa or Mike and their attempts to understand their partner's point of view. They are almost like fever dreams, existing in a space between white fragility and Black fatigue, and satirize contemporary perspectives on modern culture through pop-culture references and tropes that will be particularly familiar to Black audiences. Between these micro-plays, a cascading debate between Mike and Marissa about race and the nature of their relationship intensifies, climaxing when they have dinner with their white friend Jordan and their Black friends Gerald and Aisha. Through its hard-hitting comedic elements, *Redbone Coonhound* explores the intricacies of race, systemic power, and privilege in remarkable and surprising ways.

ABOUT THE UNDERGROUND RAILROAD

The Underground Railroad was not underground, nor was it a railroad. It was a network of clandestine routes and safe houses (which were called stations) established in the United States during the early to mid-nineteenth century. The Underground Railroad assisted enslaved African Americans in their escape to freedom, often to Northern states where slavery has been abolished. Those who guided people along the Railroad were known as conductors. The Railroad was operated by formerly enslaved Black people, free Black people, and white abolitionists, many of whom were Quakers. Oral history indicates that Indigenous Peoples in the Great Lakes region also assisted. The passage of the amended Fugitive Slave Act of 1850 required that all escaped enslaved people, upon capture, be returned to the slaver, and even in free states, officials and citizens had to cooperate or face criminal charges. This spurred some moderate abolitionists in the North to take action to defy the law, lest they be morally aligned with slavery. During this time, the Underground Railroad reached its peak of operation, and the main destination for escape was British North America (later to become Canada), where slavery had been abolished since August 1, 1834. Estimates vary widely, but at least 30,000 to 50,000 people escaped to Canada via the Underground Railroad. Some estimates put that number up to 100,000, but considering that in 1860 there were approximately 3.9 million enslaved people in the United States, the Underground Railroad was only a route to freedom for a small percentage of people. Nevertheless, it was a marvellously improvised metaphorical construct run by courageous heroes, many of whom were Black themselves, who risked their lives to save the lives of others.

ABOUT HARRIET TUBMAN

Harriet Tubman was an escaped enslaved woman who became a conductor on the Underground Railroad, leading enslaved people to freedom before the Civil War, all while carrying a bounty on her head. But she was also a nurse, a Union spy, and a women's suffrage supporter. On September 17, 1849, Harriet escaped the Maryland plantation where she had been enslaved. With the help of the Underground Railroad, Harriet persevered and travelled ninety miles north to Pennsylvania and freedom. It is believed that Harriet personally led at least seventy enslaved people to freedom, including her elderly parents, and she is estimated to have instructed over sixty others – none of whom were caught – how to escape on their own. She famously said, "I never ran my train off the track, and I never lost a passenger." She usually acted in winter months when her group would be less likely to be seen. Though she received help from white abolitionists, her missions were still incredibly treacherous, and she put herself at tremendous personal risk. She was nicknamed "Moses" by abolitionist William Lloyd Garrison because, like the Biblical Moses who led the Hebrews to freedom from Egypt, Harriet wanted nothing more than to set her people free, and she did. She was also a deeply religious woman with unshakeable faith, which was intensified by a traumatic head injury she suffered from a violent overseer. After this incident, for which she received no medical attention, she began to experience vivid dreams and powerful visions. She believed these were revelations and premonitions from God that helped keep her and those she guided safe during her trips.

ABOUT HOGAN'S ALLEY AND BLACK VANCOUVER

Early in the play, the narrator emphasizes the lack of Black people and a distinct Black community in Vancouver. This was not always the case: Vancouver once was home to Hogan's Alley, the unofficial name for a T-shaped intersection at the southwestern edge of Strathcona. The name was in use by 1914, and over the years the area became a distinctly Black neighbourhood that included cottages, makeshift night clubs, and southern-style restaurants as well as "chicken house" restaurants, such as Vie's Chicken and Steak House that also operated as a speakeasy. This establishment was well-known and well-loved within the community, and Jimi Hendrix's grandmother, Nora Hendrix, worked there as a cook. Vie's Chicken and Steak House was visited by famous jazz musicians of the time, like Louis Armstrong and Ella Fitzgerald, Sammy Davis Jr., Cab Calloway, Count Basie, Mitzi Gaynor, and Nat King Cole. Hogan's Alley was also home to the Crump Twins, who were part of one of the original Black families that had migrated from Oklahoma to Vancouver. Twins Robert and Ronnie were two young boys who loved to dance, sing, and act in many of the local places on Hogan's Alley. There were also porter clubs, like the Pullman Porter's Club, which backed onto Hogan's Alley and was patronized predominantly by Black men who worked as sleeping car porters for the railroad. Its presence connected Hogan's Alley with Black communities throughout North America by word of mouth and through organizations like the Brotherhood of Sleeping Car Porters, an organization created to advocate for Black rights.

Over the years, the Black population endured efforts by the city to rezone Strathcona, which made it difficult to obtain mortgages or carry out home improvements, and news articles slandering Hogan's Alley as a centre of squalor, immorality, and crime. Beginning in 1967, the City of Vancouver began levelling the western half of Hogan's Alley to construct an interurban freeway through Hogan's Alley and Chinatown. The freeway was ultimately stopped, but construction of the first phase – the Georgia Viaduct – was completed in 1971. In the process, the western end of Hogan's Alley was expropriated, and several blocks of houses were demolished. Since the demise of Hogan's Alley, no identifiably Black neighbourhood has emerged in Vancouver. To learn more Black history in Vancouver and view some great storytelling videos, visit blackstrathcona.com/.

ABOUT BLACK LIVES MATTER

#BlackLivesMatter, mentioned in the play, is a global organization "founded in 2013 in response to the acquittal of Trayvon Martin's murderer," inspiring a new generation of protests against police and against vigilante violence towards Black people. Their mission "is to eradicate white supremacy and build local power to intervene in violence inflicted on Black communities by by the state and vigilantes." By combating and countering acts of violence, creating space for Black imagination and innovation, and centring Black joy, BLM affirms "the lives of Black queer and trans folks, disabled folks, undocumented folks, folks with records, women, and all Black lives along the gender spectrum." It is "working for a world where Black lives are no longer systematically targeted for demise." See blacklivesmatter.com/about/.

DEFINITIONS

- Cultural appropriation: when members of a majority group adopt cultural elements of a minority group in an exploitative, disrespectful, or stereotypical way.
- Misogyny: dislike of, contempt for, or ingrained prejudice against women.
- Patriarchy: a system of society or government in which men hold the power and women are largely excluded from it.
- Systemic racism: a form of racism that is embedded in the laws and regulations of a society or an organization.
- White supremacy: a political, economic, and cultural system in which whites overwhelmingly control power and material resources, conscious and unconscious ideas of white superiority and entitlement are widespread, and relations of white dominance and non-white subordination are daily re-enacted across a broad array of institutions and social settings.
- White fragility: discomfort and defensiveness on the part of a white person when confronted by information about racial inequality and injustice.
- White privilege: inherent advantages possessed by a white person on the basis of their race in a society characterized by racial inequality and injustice.
- Woke: originating in African American Vernacular English (AAVE), to be "woke" is to be alert to racial prejudice and discrimination.

DISCUSSION QUESTIONS

These questions can be used as writing prompts, as well as prompts for group discussions.

PRE-SHOW DISCUSSION QUESTIONS

- What's your earliest memory of becoming aware of racism?
- How comfortable are you talking about race? Is it something you consider day-to-day? Why or why not?
- Have you ever felt "different" in a group setting because of your race or ethnicity? How did this affect you? If not, have you ever considered what it might feel like or why you've never felt "different"?
- What do you think of when you hear the term white supremacy?
- Do you ever feel like you might have be acting unfairly towards somebody because of their race?
- How would it make you feel if a person of colour called something you did or said racist? How would you respond?

POST-SHOW DISCUSSION QUESTIONS

These questions are ideal for engaging students in reflection and exploration of the major themes, characters, and other elements of the production.

- How do the pop culture references in this play work to engage with topics around race and racism? Did you find them funny? Why or why not?
- Consider both Mike and Marissa's perspectives throughout the play. Is there anything you relate to or find easier to understand in either of their experiences?
- How does Mike change through the play?
- Is there anything that you didn't understand about the play?
- What do you think the significance of the play's ending is?

FURTHER RESOURCES

BOOKS

Cole, Desmond. *The Skin We're In: A Year of Black Resistance and Power.* Toronto: Doubleday Canada, 2020. www.penguinrandomhouse.ca/books/536075/the-skin-were-in-by-desmond-cole/9780385686341.

hooks, bell. *We Real Cool: Black Men and Masculinity.* New York: Routledge, 2004. www.routledge.com/We-Real-Cool-Black-Men-and-Masculinity/hooks/p/book/9780415969277.

Maynard, Robyn. *Policing Black Lives: State Violence in Canada from Slavery to the Present.* Halifax: Fernwood Publishing, 2017. fernwoodpublishing.ca/book/policing-black-lives.

Winters, Mary-Frances. *Black Fatigue: How Racism Erodes the Mind, Body, and Spirit.* Oakland: Berrett-Koehler Publishers, 2020. www.penguinrandomhouse.com/books/647356/black-fatigue-by-mary-frances-winters/.

ONLINE RESOURCES

1619. Podcast. Produced by Annie Brown, Adizah Eghan, and Kelly Prime. *New York Times*, updated June 10, 2020. www.nytimes.com/2020/01/23/podcasts/1619-podcast.html.

Global Centre for Pluralism. "Talking About Racism in the Classroom." Google doc. Accessed January 18, 2024. docs.google.com/document/d/1R5LilMikICJStuu85fczoqNX07Ku0GPsjRRxwIflA-Y/edit.

Hogan's Alley Society (website). Accessed January 18, 2024. www.hogansalleysociety.org/.

National Film Board. "Black Communities in Canada." Free collection of films. National Film Board (website). Accessed January 18, 2024. www.nfb.ca/channels/black-communities-canada/?ed_en=feature_4&feature_type=playlist&banner_id=79609%20.

"Resources." Black Lives Matter (website). Accessed January 18, 2024. blacklivesmatter.com/resources/.

SOURCES

LEARNING OBJECTIVES AND BC CURRICULUM CONNECTIONS

"Critical Thinking and Reflective Thinking." BC's Curriculum (website). Accessed January 9, 2024. curriculum.gov.bc.ca/competencies/thinking /critical-and-reflective-thinking.

UNDERGROUND RAILROAD AND HARRIET TUBMAN

"Harriet Tubman, the Moses of her People." Harriet Tubman Historical Society (website). Accessed January 9, 2024. www.harriet-tubman.org /moses-underground-railroad/.

History.com Editors. "Underground Railroad." History.com. Updated March 29, 2023. www.history.com/topics/black-history /underground-railroad.

Piccotti, Tyler, and Biography.com editors. "Harriet Tubman." Biography .com. Updated December 11, 2023. www.biography.com/activist /harriet-tubman.

Gates, Henry Louis, Jr. "Who Really Ran the Underground Railroad?" PBS.org. Accessed January 9, 2024. www.pbs.org/wnet/african -americans-many-rivers-to-cross/history/who-really-ran-the -underground-railroad/.

HOGAN'S ALLEY AND BLACK VANCOUVER

BC Entertainment Hall of Fame. "The Crump Twins." BC Entertainment Hall of Fame (website). Accessed January 18, 2024. bcentertainmenthalloffame.com/crump-twins/.

Black Strathcona. "Sleeping Car Porters." Accessed January 18, 2024. YouTube video, 2:14. www.youtube.com/watch?v=yq_RIGbJnOE.

Compton, Wayde. "Hogan's Alley." *The Canadian Encyclopedia*. Last edited February 14, 2019. www.thecanadianencyclopedia.ca/en/article /hogans-alley.

Creative Cultural Collaboration Society. Black Strathcona (website). 2014. www.blackstrathcona.com.

Hogan's Alley Society (website). Accessed January 18, 2024. www
.hogansalleysociety.org/.

Rudder, Adam. "Hogan's Alley: The making of a black community in
Vancouver." Rabble.ca. February 18, 2014. rabble.ca/anti-racism
/hogans-alley-making-black-community-vancouver/.

Vancouver Heritage Foundation. "Hogan's Alley." Places That Matter:
Community History Resource (website). 2024. placesthatmatter.ca
/location/hogans-alley/.

ABOUT BLACK LIVES MATTER AND DEFINITIONS

"About." Black Lives Matter (website). Accessed January 18, 2024.
blacklivesmatter.com/about/.

Bustle Editors and Kaitlyn Wylde. "There's More To 'Woke' Than You
Think." Bustle (website). Updated January 6, 2022. www.bustle.com/life
/what-does-woke-mean-theres-more-to-the-slang-term-than-you-think.

Harold, Laura. "What Is White Fragility?" Very Well Mind (website).
Updated January 03, 2023. www.verywellmind.com/white-fragility
-4847115.

Sheppard, Colleen, Tamara Thermitus, and Derek J. Jones. "Understanding
How Racism Becomes Systemic." McGill Centre for Human Rights and
Legal Pluralism (website). August 18, 2020. www.mcgill.ca/humanrights
/article/universal-human-rights/understanding-how-racism-becomes
-systemic.